PRAISE
SEVEN FREEDOM
ELEMENTS

"The seven freedom elements presented in this liberating book are clearly the result of many hours of coaching experience and research. It's very insightful, easy to read, and extremely practical in understanding how to live an awakened life around your career, relationships, or life more generally. If you want to end the struggle and embrace confidence, joy and freedom, read this book (and give a copy to your team as well!)"

– Avril Carpenter, Hypnotherapist

"I wish I'd found this book 20 years ago! As someone who has spent the last two decades working out how to live a life of freedom, I can promise you that Seven Freedom Elements sets out exactly what you need to know to take back control of your life and start creating the results you want. I particularly love what Kylie shares about Element 6 (Responsibility), which she aptly calls your "superpower"; that was the piece that really turned my world right side up. If there's anything you want to change about your life, Seven Freedom Elements will give you the insights and strategies to make it happen."

– Caroline New, Executive Coach, Quantum Values

"Seven Freedom Elements is a roadmap towards personal freedom. This book provides valuable insights and tips on how to take control of your life on all levels. It is a guide on how to attain true emancipation from, often imaginary, ties that hold you back from living a truly unencumbered and liberated life. Seven Freedom Elements is outstanding in its simplicity and punctuated with real-life examples, making it a comfortable, entertaining and enlightening read. I couldn't put it down. And it has become my new go-to manual for the times when I am feeling restrained or held back by something or someone, imaginary or real. As a self-confessed self-help book enthusiast, if there was one book in this genre I would recommend, Seven Freedom Elements would be it. Do yourself a favour and invest in your own journey to personal freedom."

– Annette Guilfoyle, Executive Manager

SEVEN FREEDOM ELEMENTS

SEVEN FREEDOM ELEMENTS

**The Essential Foundations
for Confidence, Clarity
and a Life You Love**

KYLIE ZEAL

NEW YORK

NASHVILLE • MELBOURNE • VANCOUVER

Seven Freedom Elements

The Essential Foundations for Confidence, Clarity and a Life You Love

© 2018 Kylie Zeal

Published in New York, New York, by Morgan James Publishing. Morgan James is a trademark of Morgan James, LLC. www.MorganJamesPublishing.com

The Morgan James Speakers Group can bring authors to your live event. For more information or to book an event visit The Morgan James Speakers Group at www.TheMorganJamesSpeakersGroup.com.

ISBN 9781683505372 paperback
ISBN 9781683505389 eBook
Library of Congress Control Number: 2017905454

Cover Design by:
Julia Kuris
www.designerbility.com.au

Interior Design by:
Chris Treccani
www.3dogcreative.net

In an effort to support local communities, raise awareness and funds, Morgan James Publishing donates a percentage of all book sales for the life of each book to Habitat for Humanity Peninsula and Greater Williamsburg.

Get involved today! Visit
www.MorganJamesBuilds.com

CONTENTS

*For Hannah, Lexi,
Erin and Reina*

*Every time I take myself on,
no matter how scary, and
regardless of the outcome, a
new trajectory for the rest of
my life is created.*

PREFACE

The first seeds of this book were sown about fourteen years ago.

Sitting in the little cubicle waiting for my next student, I wondered a little nervously about what to expect. I was teaching English in Japan and students were normally allocated randomly to teachers, but Rie had specifically asked to see me again.

I remembered the last time we met. We were halfway through a lesson about travel, practising all the generic phrases such as, "What will the weather be like?" when I could no longer resist the feeling that something was wrong. Though I didn't know her, I sensed that something weighed heavily on her mind.

I looked her in the eyes and asked, "Are you okay? You seem distracted or concerned about something."

In her broken English, she said, "My work is trouble."

For the remainder of the lesson, I asked Rie thought-provoking questions about her work situation. We explored what she thought was the worst that could happen and what she would do if it ever actually happened, all the while practising her English.

So now, three weeks later, I sat in the same cubicle where we had met before. Rie entered, put her books on the table, sat down and looked at me. She paused, perhaps trying to gather her words in English, then said, "Last time you help me with my work. You ask me about the worst thing."

"Yes," I responded.

"Teach me again," she said.

I did teach Rie again and she left happy. I felt happy too. It lit me up to know that someone had turned up with the weight of a challenge and left feeling much lighter, happier and empowered. It felt amazing to have played a role in that. Perhaps that should have been all the evidence I needed to know that I had something of value to offer. Perhaps right then I should have simply accepted that I had gifts and insights and turned it into a business so that I could help more people create the life they wanted.

The reality was it would be another ten years of experiences, challenging myself, education, therapy and coaching before I would know beyond doubt that I brought something of value to my work, my life and the world. And while all that time I had a strong feeling about the book I wanted to write, I see retrospectively that the book could only evolve as fast as I did.

What I learned during those ten years was how to create a level of personal freedom that had not previously existed, even in my imagination.

A decade earlier, I didn't even have a sense of self, let alone a sense of personal freedom. So much of my identity was connected to the people I spent time with, especially whoever I was in a relationship with at the time. So much of what I did was tied to what I thought was expected of me or what I felt I deserved (which was not much).

My self-worth was low. I used to have panic attacks and I was diagnosed with Post Traumatic Stress Disorder at one point. I recall times when I was a very low-functioning version of a human being, if not completely incapacitated by the personal reality in which I resided.

This journey to personal freedom took a lot of courage and healing, and it all took time.

Occasionally, it was a battle – an internal one that inevitably played out externally as well, as demonstrated one day when I found myself yelling at my singing teacher, "My voice just can't sing like that!"

About six weeks earlier, a friend had called and asked if I'd sing at her wedding. The voice in my head said, "No, are you crazy? Of course I can't sing at your wedding!" I loved to sing and we'd been to karaoke a number of times, but this seemed crazy. Singing was a daydream, fantasy thing for me, more suited to other people with real singing talent.

I would have politely declined the flattering invitation, but the never-happy-no-matter-what-you-do voice in my mind said, *'You're a coach and you are always coaching people to do the things they're afraid of. If you don't do this then you're a fraud!'*

Whoa! A fraud? I knew feeling like a fraud would be even harder for me to live with than the fear of looking like a fool, so I said to my friend, "Okay, I'd be happy to sing at your wedding." I think she believed me.

After I hung up the phone, I just stood there, not quite sure what to do with myself. I was stunned and even felt nauseated as

I played out all of the possible embarrassing scenarios involving singing at a wedding. Who was I kidding? I was *not* a good singer. She must have been desperate when she asked me to sing; I must have been arrogant to think I could.

This was a moment of choice. I could call my friend back and tell her I wasn't feeling comfortable with the idea of singing. She would understand. I, however, would be less understanding because I knew the truth: If I said "no", I would be running away because I was afraid. So instead of picking up the phone, I went to my computer and searched for singing teachers in my area.

The singing teacher I found was wonderful, though you wouldn't have thought so from the way I'd just yelled at her. My friend had chosen the song *Amazing Grace* and though I'd been to several singing lessons already and had practised endlessly, my voice kept breaking at the end of the second line whenever I sang it in my singing teacher's way. My voice didn't break like that when I did it *my* way. If I messed up the performance, I would feel so embarrassed! I was annoyed at myself for having agreed to sing at all.

When I yelled, "My voice just can't sing like that!" without even flinching, my teacher shot back at me, "It can and it will."

I was stunned by her conviction and her unwavering faith in my ability to sing. Speechless, I thought, *'She must know something I don't.'*

I surrendered. I listened as she explained the breaking in my voice was due to a lack of practice. My vocal chords were stronger up high and down low, but the middle was rarely used so it was weak. We practised scales regularly (they actually do have a purpose!). I also practised at home and in the car. Every moment in between, I did my best to have faith that it was working.

By the day of the wedding, my voice was no longer breaking. I still felt nervous, but I was as ready as I was ever going to be.

An honest appraisal of my singing at the wedding is that it was okay. I received some wonderful compliments from several people later in the day and the bride was happy. It was a beautiful wedding and a privilege to have played a role. Even though I knew my singing could have been better, it didn't matter. The result didn't really matter to me. All that mattered was who I had been and how I felt.

I felt free.

I'd taken on my internal battle and I'd won!

Everything I have created since has occurred in the trajectory created by that moment. It's how life works. Every time I take myself on, no matter how scary, and regardless of the outcome, a new trajectory for the rest of my life is created. That's why these moments of personal triumph are so important. This was one of those moments.

This book was finished in that moment.

Of course, I still had hundreds of hours of writing, learning, frustration and hard work ahead of me, but that was just the physical world catching up with the reality that now existed in my mind...

I am free to create anything I want.

I am free to be whoever I want.

I am free.

Of course, my self-development journey is not over and never will be. I still get challenged regularly, but I know where to go and what to do to bring myself back to a state of peace and freedom. Sometimes I am pleasantly surprised at how quickly I can go from a state of anxiety to peace, and I think, *'How awesome is that?'* It might not be instantaneous. It might take me several hours or more to really bring myself back, depending on what has knocked me from my centre. Yet even this feels like an unbelievable improvement when compared to how I used to be.

For everything I learn about myself, humans and life, I realise there is a lot more about which I don't even have a clue. But I am very excited to have reached the stage where I could write this book. I knew I was ready because the words began to flow and I could see what was previously unimaginable.

In writing this book, I've stopped taking my insights about freedom, which come so naturally to me these days, for granted. I want to share it with others who seek the same because it would bring me no greater joy than to know I have contributed to their personal freedom.

For more than ten years, I've felt that joy and celebrated every time my clients and others create more freedom for themselves. For someone to take themselves on for the sake of freedom requires courage and commitment, and to be invited to bear witness feels to me like a privilege and a gift. Their courage inspires me to be courageous. So if you're ready for more freedom in your life, then you're in the right place. And if you'd like to share your stories of courage and personal freedom, I would love to receive them. You can contact me via my website: www.SevenFreedomElements.com.

Here's to creating a level of freedom that you're yet to even imagine,

Kylie

"All the significant battles are waged within the self."

– Sheldon Kopp

Personal freedom means you live by the code of your inner voice.

INTRODUCTION

Maybe you can create life changes tomorrow. It's not possible today, right? Too busy. Not enough time. Not enough money. Not enough help available. Not smart enough. Not thin enough. Not fit enough. Not confident enough.

This track, or at least your own variation of it, keeps playing in your mind and you know it well. It somehow seems to blend in perfectly with the external track you keep hearing on repeat. You know, the one that says, *'Be nice, look good and do it all.'* It's the track you've heard all your life about who you're supposed to be. Occasionally there's a different verse. Sometimes it's, *'Look sexy'* or *'Be perfect'* or *'Be smart.'* Then the chorus cuts in again – *'Be nice, look good and do it all.'* You thought the tune might change once you got that degree or got married. But that same track keeps on playing. You wondered if it would change when you had children, or when you got the promotion, or when you started your own business. But like a broken record, or perhaps a pounding headache, the track plays on... '*Be nice, look good, do it all.*'

On some level, you know this is not supposed to be the soundtrack to your life. But you fear, like a game of musical chairs, that if the music stops, everyone will find a chair before you and you'll be the one left standing... all alone... while everyone else stares.

Still, in those quiet moments, you hear and see something different for your life. If only you could discover how to make changes and set yourself free to create what you really want.

What is personal freedom?

Personal freedom means you live by the code of your inner voice. You regularly take time to quiet the chatter of your mind and tune in to your intuitive sense of who you are and how you most want to live your life. And even though your inner wisdom often calls you to do things that scare you, you trust you can create the vision it has shown you.

You might not always know what steps to take next and you might be judged for your actions, but having personal freedom means you are not paralysed by judgements, nor do you apologise for living your truth. You have the courage and strength to keep going, or to reach out for the hand that is offering assistance. You take chances, stretch yourself and bear the inevitable pain that comes with the growth and personal transformations you pursue. Like the caterpillar that leaves its old self behind and struggles through transformation, you know to keep pushing through the resistance. You know that the strength developed through your struggles will manifest the ability to fly.

Personal freedom means you allow yourself to soar. For as much courage as it took for you to keep moving through resistance and to find the strength when your challenges seemed insurmountable, an even greater amount of courage is required to embrace the magnificence that exists within you.

Personal freedom means you can let go. Your empowered self is not dependent on any one person, community, thing or thought. Your free self attracts some people and causes others to leave. It doesn't matter. You know that neither enhances nor diminishes the universal truth that everything is connected. You can courageously feel the pain of loss when you need to, and allow those feelings of loss to enhance rather than diminish you.

Personal freedom means you embrace life. It means you love, both gently and fiercely. Free from fear of loss, you feel abundant. Your ability to deeply connect with others is a natural result of your freedom to have a deep, loving connection with yourself. You nurture and nourish yourself. You seek intimacy. You forgive yourself for mistakes and your connection with your humanity is a connection with all humanity. Through it all, you are free, at liberty to simply be whoever you choose to be.

Getting what you really want

In over a decade of specialising in personal development, I've found there are certain areas in particular where people want to experience freedom:

Confidence

Clients often have coaching goals to 'be more confident' or 'more assertive'. They would like to be able to speak up without trembling. They want to be able to ask for the things they need in such a way that their message is heard. And they want to move forward in life and claim those things they desire and know they deserve.

Developing your freedom elements creates confidence.

Quality relationships

All clients, without exception, want quality relationships. For some, this means a 'partnership' or being 'committed'. For others it means 'healthy' or 'loving' or 'fun' relationships. We want to feel understood and connected to others, especially those most important to us. We also want to feel safe and free to be our most authentic selves within our relationships.

Developing your freedom elements improves the quality of your relationships.

Health

Health is important to many clients I work with. They understand that good health will assist them in creating the other things they really want in their life. Some want to lose weight or be stronger or improve their energy levels or the way they look. Others want to ensure they are doing what they can to live the longest and healthiest life possible.

Developing your freedom elements improves your health.

Successful career or business

Most clients aspire to do work every day that they enjoy as well as providing them with the financial means to purchase things they think would add value to their lives. Some want to build a business or get a promotion or have greater flexibility to do the things that are important to them, such as spending time with family. Some want to do work they feel makes a difference or contributes to the lives of others.

Developing your freedom elements creates career opportunities, flexibility and success.

Finances

Many clients want to improve the state of their finances. They may want more money or to be better at managing the money they have. They are also keen to have a more empowering attitude about money and remove the mental and emotional blocks to creating wealth.

Developing your freedom elements creates clarity and empowerment in the area of finances.

Happiness

Some clients directly declare, "I want to be happier." Others express their desire for greater happiness with statements such as, "I want more work/life balance," or "I need to work out what I really want," or "I want to feel more relaxed," or "I just want to be me."

Developing your freedom elements creates more happiness.

The seven freedom elements

It's time to set yourself free.

It's time to let go of all the rules about how you should look or behave and to rise above all of the judgements you encounter endlessly from yourself and others.

From a place of freedom you can create anything you want and be an inspiration for other to do the same.

How can you claim your personal freedom? You need to develop your seven freedom elements.

Element 1: Self-knowledge

Self-knowledge is about knowing who you are and why you behave the way you do. It's about understanding what makes you human and what makes you a unique individual. It's the first freedom element because to create freedom, you first need to be able to see where you are not free.

Element 2: Meaning

Your reality is determined by the meanings you create about it. Fortunately, you can choose the meanings you create. The quality of your life will be determined by the quality of those meanings.

Element 3: Self-worth

Self-worth is the decision you make about your value. It is a decision that can only be made by you and cannot be determined by anything external to you. By acknowledging your self-worth, you will bring into your life what you believe you deserve.

Element 4: Energy

As you pursue your freedom and anything else you are passionate about, you will inevitably experience resistance. The only way to overcome this force is to create even greater levels of mind and body energy within you.

Element 5: Calm

Much of the chatter in your mind is not useful and is a barrier to your sense of freedom. Cultivating a sense of calm will increase your levels of clarity, empathy, love, confidence, courage and creativity, as well as your experience of freedom.

Element 6: Responsibility

Responsibility is your superpower! You always have a choice about how you respond to what happens in life. When you choose to take responsibility for your actions and outcomes, you can create anything. You are that powerful.

Element 7: Courage

Courage allows you to take risks and to let go of the things that don't serve you. It empowers you to keep moving forward in spite of knowing that nothing is certain. It empowers you to pursue personal freedom.

As you understand, practice and implement these elements, your freedom expands.

The seven elements all interact with each other. For instance, self-knowledge draws heavily on both courage and responsibility, while meaning and responsibility are also closely linked. I've made all mentions of the elements that appear in different chapters in bold to help highlight this relationship, so you can see examples of how they all connect.

The connection between the elements means that simply improving on one element will have a positive impact on the others. Likewise, if you're weak in one area, this will also impact the others. It reminds me of Trivial Pursuit, the board game my parents bought for our family when I was a child. Each player has to make their way around the board with a circular, plastic piece that contains six triangular spaces. If I wanted to win the game, I needed to fill each of these spaces with a different-coloured triangle (or 'piece of pie' as we called them). Each colour represents a different category of questions. When I was a kid, I had a preference for the pink (entertainment) or orange (sports and leisure) categories. I seemed to get more of these answers correct and each time I got a question right, I got another turn, which meant more opportunities to land on the squares that rewarded pieces of pie. If I could have won the game by filling my pie with all pink and orange pieces, I probably would have done so. But that is not how you win the game. You have to demonstrate strength in all six categories.

Creating a life of freedom is like attempting to win a game of Trivial Pursuit – while you will notice improvements in your life if you develop some of the elements, to experience true freedom you have to develop them all.

The seven freedom elements are organised in the order that makes most sense to me. However, the chapters do not need to be read in order. If you feel most drawn to read about self-worth or energy or one of the other elements, you are welcome to go right ahead and read about them now, knowing that whichever elements you develop will have a positive impact overall and contribute to your life of freedom.

Who am I to write about freedom?

Most of all, I write about creating a life of freedom because I know what it's like to live without it. I know what it's like to love too much (which I've since learned is more fear than love), to constantly second guess myself, to give up my own needs for the needs of others, to fear rejection, to live small and to believe that this is as good as it gets.

I was so wrong.

Before I discovered how wrong I was, I had a career in finance. It was a practical career choice and my family and friends all approved. But finance was never my passion. Sure, those business skills have often come in handy, but finance was not the career I would have pursued if I was living authentically.

Fortunately, my life fell apart. Of course it didn't feel so fortunate at the time. But I have since come to see very clearly the upside of one of the most challenging times in my life – when I felt like I had lost everything I also believed I had nothing to lose. So I took what felt like a big risk and enrolled in a Social Science degree. I chose to major in Psychology and Sociology because that's what inspired me.

I loved it! I loved going to lectures about the human mind and I was fascinated by human behaviour. Around the same time, I also discovered a passion for coaching – there was something about positive psychology that really resonated with me. Not wanting to wait until I completed my degree to get started, I undertook an Advanced Practitioner of Coaching certification.

When I completed both qualifications, I took another leap of faith and began my own coaching practice. This freaked me out! I was so far out of my comfort zone and the only thing that stopped me from quitting was my integrity – I believed I was not fit to coach people to do things they were afraid of if I wasn't prepared to take on my own fears. So leap I did, and to my amazement and gratitude, I discovered that the universe had my back – I learned that if I continue showing up, people will be engaged and inspired and life will keep throwing me opportunities. My business took off and my experience of freedom expanded.

My coaching experience led to managing a two-year research project looking at the benefits of coaching for a group of young adults with cystic fibrosis. Leading a team of seven coaches who worked with sixty coaching clients, we were able to provide evidence of the difference coaching can make. Namely, coaching can increase an individual's motivation to stick to their prescribed health regimen and improve quality of life. Given the biggest contributing factor to how long someone with cystic fibrosis can live is their adherence to a demanding health regimen (the usual diet and exercise routine the rest of us should follow pales in comparison), this was a very rewarding project to be involved in. I felt I made a valuable contribution to the cystic fibrosis community, including my five-year-old nephew who has this condition.

Once the project was completed, I started teaching coaching skills all over Australia. I followed that by combining my coaching and business skills and focusing on executive coaching, working with leaders and their teams. I accumulated a lot of training and coaching hours, enough to be recognised by the International Coach Federation as a Professional Certified Coach.

My work over the last decade has been more rewarding and fulfilling than I could have imagined, and it was only possible because I continued to take myself on again and again - especially when I was freaking out! Managing my internal state, regardless of what is happening around me, is the only way to really experience freedom. I also see this in everyone I work with – CEOs, school principals, entrepreneurs, health practitioners and many other professionals who come to understand that true freedom comes from within and is not tied to external success.

If you want to enhance your experience of freedom, follow in the footsteps of my clients and journey with me through the seven freedom elements.

"Consciously or not, we are all on a quest for answers, trying to learn the lessons of life. We grapple with fear and guilt. We search for meaning, love, and power. We try to understand fear, loss, and time. We seek to discover who we are and how we can become truly happy."

– Elisabeth Kubler-Ross

*We must choose
self-awareness, or risk lives of
denial and self-sabotage.*

ELEMENT 1:

Self-knowledge

I was twenty-seven years old and I wanted my life to be better.

My career wasn't working. Though it paid good money and I enjoyed the work and the people I worked with, I wasn't passionate about it and that left me feeling drained. My relationship had also ended and I was heartbroken. I thought my life was planned out; I was going to marry that person, settle down and live a normal, happy life. Instead, I felt completely lost and that I was failing at life.

The only upside I could see at the time was that I wasn't tied to anything. So when an opportunity presented itself to work in Japan, the decision to go was effortless. I felt I needed to do some soul searching. I also knew I wanted more free time. So much of my life had been filled with busyness. I rarely took the time to remind myself why I was doing all of the things that made me so busy.

Was I actually thinking for myself? Or was I simply going after certain things that other people told me were important? This seemed to lead to more existential questions like, 'Who am I?', 'What do I really want out of life?' and 'Have I ever really learned to think for myself?'

Aristotle once said, "Knowing yourself is the beginning of all wisdom." If Aristotle had been alive and had any inclination to give consideration to my identity crisis, he would not have chosen me as the poster-child for wisdom, but he likely would have supported my soul-searching expedition.

I took a job teaching English part-time because I knew I'd find it easy and it would give me lots of free time. You could say I took the concept of soul searching seriously. I spent a lot of my time just walking around Japan being open to experiences as well as being introspective. I also read and listened to a lot of books. I was particularly interested in books by people who thought in ways that were different from me and who seemed to enjoy life more than I did. I sensed they knew something I didn't and I wanted to know what it was.

One thing I learned was they had a much better understanding of themselves than I did. They had insight about where they were keeping themselves trapped and how to set themselves free. There also seemed to be a common theme in the belief that the life we experience is a reflection of our thoughts. I resonated with many of the concepts they shared, such as the idea that I am responsible for how I experience the world.

But I was often challenged by how to implement what I learned. This would always lead to more self-discovery about why I felt challenged. I needed to be aware of all of the beliefs I had about myself and life in order to see the connection between them and the life I was creating. Eventually, I would either find ways to implement what I was learning, or I would find myself in a situation that forced me to.

Giving myself the time for unfettered self-discovery was one of the best decisions I ever made. It afforded me the opportunity to create a whole new foundation from which to discover myself and grow. I've never since allocated such an extended period of time to self-discovery, but I do make time for introspection and seek feedback regularly because I have learned the power of those insights. It was, in hindsight, a pivotal decision because it enabled me to fulfil the wish of my twenty-seven-year-old self... life got better.

> *"And you? When will you begin that long journey into yourself?"*
>
> **– Rumi**

> *"Any human being who is becoming independent of conditionings, of religions, scriptures, prophets and messiahs, has arrived home. He has found the treasure which was hidden in his own being."*
>
> **– Osho**

Are you willing to look inside?

Self-knowledge is the first key to unlocking your freedom. To be free, you first must see where you are not free.

Self-knowledge means you are willing to honestly look at yourself – your strengths and weaknesses, successes and failures, how you behave under pressure and where there's opportunity to improve.

This can be challenging. Any serious journey of self-exploration will bring up uncomfortable or painful feelings – just think of the last time you had to apologise to someone. You first had to be willing to admit that you were wrong and caused harm. And then you had to acknowledge it to another person. Ouch!

When there is a risk of pain or discomfort, most people will go to great lengths to convince themselves that there is no problem. Who can blame them? We all know how much it can hurt when someone criticises or disapproves of us – especially if we value their opinion. So it's not surprising that we adopt ways of hiding our 'unacceptable' parts from the world and from ourselves. We choose to deceive ourselves.

A common example of self-deception is avoiding looking at your credit card statements. Danielle, one of my coaching clients, struggled with this. She knew she wouldn't have the money to pay off the account in full and she decided that was all she needed to know. She paid what she could and then carried on with life, enjoying the reprieve provided by the illusion that there was no problem.

Danielle knew deep down, if she chose to be aware of the extent to which her credit card account was out of control, she would have to take responsibility for changing it. This was where she got stuck – instead of examining her behaviour, she decided not to look because then she didn't need to do anything differently. Everything she tried in the past had failed, and she predicted looking any closer at the issue would just confirm she was a failure.

Guided self-exploration was a positive turning point for Danielle. She was able to see the credit card statements were just a symptom. Through coaching, we discovered that the real issue was Danielle's low self-worth. She didn't feel valuable and she compensated by buying clothes and other items she couldn't really afford. Danielle also questioned whether she had the skills or ability to take control of the debt and turn it around. However, before she could deal with any of these core issues, she first had to be willing to look at them.

Another client, Adriana, had been avoiding a difficult conversation with her boss, who she thought was a bully. Whether or not her boss was a bully was not the issue – as long as Adriana remained attached to that meaning, she could avoid looking at herself and all the ways she had co-created the relationship. By deceiving herself and putting her focus on her boss's behaviour, Adriana could ignore her self-doubts and lack of courage to engage in the difficult conversation.

Guided self-exploration highlighted for Adriana that she had never learned how to be assertive without being confrontational, so she would instead be passive. She also came to see how her silence was indirectly teaching her boss how to treat her. Furthermore, the resentment Adriana felt meant that she was less effective at her work, which possibly triggered her boss's attitude towards her. While none of the self-exploration was about making the boss's behaviour acceptable, it did provide Adriana with a number of valuable insights about how she was also responsible for their relationship issues and where she had the most power to create change.

For Danielle, Adriana, and even you and me, there is method in our madness. We believe we can avoid the pain by not looking at the issue and refusing to challenge ourselves. In the end though, it's still madness because it's a futile attempt to create the freedom we crave.

We must choose self-awareness, or risk lives of denial and self-sabotage where we prevent ourselves from being free and living our potential.

"To perceive is to suffer."

– Aristotle

It's astonishing how many ways we can deceive ourselves. Doctor Neel Burton wrote an entire book about it.[1] He listed thirty-eight ways, including denial, repression, vagueness, inauthenticity, intellectualisation, humour and projection – to name just a few!

Self-deception, intentional or not, is an epidemic in our world, so it's hardly surprising if you have caught it.

It has a high cost though – your freedom.

"A person prone to self-deception has a limited grasp on the truth and a restricted ability to reason, as a result of which he often makes suboptimal life choices; he also suffers from a range of psychological disturbances that remove him from tranquillity and happiness, and is impoverished and even dehumanised by a constricted range of thoughts and emotions."

– Neel Burton

Understanding who you are

In this chapter (and throughout this book), I challenge you to explore – the more you examine your inner world and who you are within your outer world, the more you will know yourself.

This is a challenging undertaking for anyone doing it earnestly. Doctor Burton, aware of the impact on people seeking greater levels of self-knowledge, warns that although his book is not intellectually demanding, it can at times be emotionally challenging, "especially for those who have seldom had the time, strength, humility, or misfortune to examine their deepest thoughts and feelings." My own experience of self-exploration, and of assisting clients with their journey, confirms Burton's contention that such exploration is not for the faint-hearted.

Don't let this stop you. Becoming self-aware is crucial to creating a life of freedom and the cost of self-deception is too great. As Carl Jung said, "Until you make the unconscious conscious, it will direct your life and you will call it fate."

In other words, until you consciously choose to be aware, you will not see how your thoughts and beliefs create your reality.

Did you know that's what happens? Do you see the connection between the thoughts you have in your mind and the results you are getting in your life?

Will your future be a fate determined by your unconscious mind? Or will you consciously choose to know yourself and create the life you want?

You have the capacity to take on the challenge of living a conscious life and not only survive the discomfort, but also find joy and inner riches that you didn't even know were possible.

"Going forward will cost you. Progress and personal growth always do. It may cost cherished beliefs you thought could protect you or show you a way out. It will cost you the 'self' you've been to become who you want to be."

– David Schnarch

What will we be exploring on this journey together?

You are so complex – every human is – and the extent to which you can explore yourself is infinite. However, in all my work with clients, I see common themes and some shared self-knowledge gaps. These are the focus of this chapter.

We'll look at the element of self-knowledge from two distinct but complementary perspectives. I'll discuss what it means to be human – the things that make you like everyone else – and how your human tendencies can impact your sense of freedom. Then we'll explore what it means to be you – the things that make you unique – and how your experiences to date led you to become who you are.

Being human

Often, in coaching, a client will reveal behaviours or habits that don't support their goals or freedom, but are quite natural given their humanity.

I respond to their revelations with, "Congratulations, you're human." It's a way of acknowledging their behaviour is normal, even if it hasn't given them the results they want. The fact is, they have responded the way most any human with the same level of self-knowledge and life experience would in the same situation.

Guess what? You are also human!

We both know you're an individual and there is no one else like you. That's true. At the same time, there are aspects to being human that make you just like everybody else! Understanding what these things are can help you understand why you do the things you do, many of which get in the way of you living your most authentic and free life.

"A surgeon who learns his or her surgery anywhere in the world can successfully operate on any human being, regardless of culture, race, nationality, language, age, occupation, religious affiliation, or political persuasion, because hearts, heads, and other parts of the anatomy will always be in relatively the same place."

– Virginia Satir

The map in your head

As human beings, we all have a metaphorical map in our heads. We use it to navigate the world in which we live. When you are born, your map has very little on it. As you move through your childhood, information is added to your map. Your experiences, culture, socialisation, family and all the people you meet have an influence and add details to your map.

You need this map to help manage all of the sensory information you are confronted with in every moment of your waking life. All your senses – sight, hearing, touch, smell and taste – are receptors for information. While your brain takes this all in, it doesn't give full attention to processing every piece of information it receives. That would take too much time and energy.

Imagine a world in which everything you encountered was inexplicable, confusing and unlike anything you had ever known. For example, imagine that every time you walked to the edge of a road, it was like the first time you had ever done it. The traffic would be terrifying. To avoid this happening, your brain creates mental structures or short cuts, called schemas, as part of your map. Your schemas contain knowledge and impressions based on your experiences. These short cuts assist with organising the information you know about the world, enable you to operate on autopilot and are also a filter you apply to situations you encounter throughout life.

When you arrive at the side of a road, your brain reviews your map and all of your schemas until it finds one that relates to the current situation. We'll call it your 'crossing the road' schema. Once identified, your brain uses it to guide your actions – look both ways, listen and watch out for cars. This entire process takes less than a second.

Your 'crossing the road' schema was created when you were a child. Once you successfully crossed the road a number of times, given not much changed during those experiences, the short cut was approved for regular use.

Now think about all the other short cuts, rules and beliefs you put on your map as a child. Back then, the world was only as big as your home, the homes of the people you knew and perhaps your school, local park and shops. Your experiences at the time taught you how to behave in order to be happy. You probably took on rules such as, 'Don't speak to strangers', 'Don't hit my brother or I'll get into trouble', (or the alternative rule: 'Make sure my parents aren't watching when I hit my brother',), 'I must eat my dinner if I want dessert', 'I must not fall over if I don't want the other kids to laugh at me', 'I feel hurt if other kids don't want to play with me', and 'Mum and Dad hold the power'.

By the time you reached seven years old, your map was largely formed and quite full of schemas and rules that were relevant to your experiences as a child. As you age, your map continues to develop, though rarely as much as is necessary. To keep your map completely up to date requires regular evaluation and self-exploration. Without this, the validity of your map will likely be, at least in part, outdated and irrelevant. This is a common problem for humans! I see it often in coaching – clients in their thirties, forties, fifties and older who are navigating the world with the same map they created as a child!

How far are you going to get in life with an outdated map?

Not far. The experience is like trying to explore New York while using a map of Sydney or London.

You go round in circles, feeling lost, and wondering why you can't get to where you want to go. You feel frustrated. Then you find yourself attempting to move faster and panicking because you sense you are running out of time. An outdated map does not enable you to live effectively. It is a hindrance to creating a sense of freedom and can even be dangerous.

Consider what happens if you're in a situation that looks similar to one you've encountered previously, but which is actually different. The brain might register the current situation as a familiar one and then apply a short cut that is inappropriate. For example, the 'crossing the road' schema becomes a hazard if you visit a country where cars are driven on the opposite side of the road from your home country. The situation feels familiar in so many ways but is radically different in at least one key aspect. You might default to your 'crossing the road' schema and get hit by a car if you are not paying attention and instinctively looking for cars in the direction they normally travel at home.

It would be nice to think we're always alert and conscious of what we're doing; that we wouldn't get hit by a car for doing something as simple as looking in the wrong direction. However, we often function on autopilot, especially in today's fast-paced society, which means we run the risk of applying old rules to new situations.

Some of the rules on your map might be from events you experienced only once, particularly if the event was intensely emotional. Most people have childhood experiences that upset, embarrassed or hurt them. My client Simone remembers the promise her dad made to take her on an excursion she was really looking forward to. She had been excitedly thinking about it every day until the date arrived and her father said he would no longer be able to take her. Simone added a rule to her map that day about not trusting what people say so she wouldn't end up disappointed. Another client, Tracy, felt that her perfectionist tendencies were related to critical comments her mother made to her as a child. She was criticised for the five marks she missed on a school test, rather than celebrating the ninety-five per cent she got right and this devastated her. When exploring her map, Tracy could see she had a rule dictating that she needed to be perfect if she wanted the approval of others. In both of these cases, even though it was a one-off experience, the emotional impact was significant enough to have a lasting effect.

> *"We cannot say that if a child is badly nourished he will become a criminal. We must see what conclusion the child has drawn."*
>
> **– Alfred Adler**

Outdated map versus current reality

To further understand the implications of an outdated map, ask yourself: How long is a human child dependent on parents and other adults for survival?

I ask this question in some of my training sessions and get a variety of responses. Some people will respond with "four" or "twelve" or "sixteen years", and I can always count on someone in the room to answer jokingly, "Thirty-five years," or "Forever!" We all have a laugh and then I remind them that while we often rely on our parents for assistance throughout our lives, this is not the same as needing them for survival. For a significant part of your early life, however, you do depend on other people for your survival. Exactly how long that is will vary from one culture to another.

The reality for all young children is this: 'If these grownups do not approve of me, love me and look after me, I will die.' The child might not think about it in exactly those terms. As young children, we don't fully comprehend the concept of death and how final it is. But young children certainly know that if they don't get fed they will be hungry, if someone hits them it will hurt, and grown-ups have all the power in a world where they are smaller than most people around them. Sure, children throw tantrums sometimes and test boundaries, perhaps even literally biting the hand that feeds them. But we all know the look of fear on a child's face when they're out in public and think they've lost their parent – fear is an appropriate response when you perceive your survival is at risk.

Fast forward a couple of decades or more and a rule such as, 'If people don't approve of me, I will die,' is no longer relevant. That is an outdated map.

As an adult, you are no longer dependent on anyone else for your survival. You probably have a job, can drive a car and pay your bills. You might manage staff and even raise children of your own. No matter what challenges you encounter, you have the resources to take them on. It might not always feel like it. Self-doubt can creep in when you are pushing yourself to grow or become something more. Sometimes your situation dictates that someone else pays bills for you or you rely on them in some other way. But if you really needed to support yourself, you would find a way. You are all you need and your survival is not dependent upon anybody else. That's your current reality.

Of course you know this. Most of the time, when life is going smoothly, you know you this. When you're in the middle of a challenge and are working with an outdated map, you'll likely feel uncertain or anxious or even panic at times. While you might not actually be in a life-threatening situation, an outdated map means you risk connecting a current event to your need for survival. When you perceive your survival is threatened, you automatically engage your fight or flight response. This is your body going into panic mode – diverting all of your energy away from your immune, digestive and reproductive systems in order to activate the mental alertness and stamina to either fight or run away from the threat. As a part of this response, you might experience sweating, your heart pounding, shaking, faster breathing and nausea. In milder cases, you might just feel anxious and unable to relax.

The fight or flight response is one of the miracles of being human. When I think about how quickly the body activates this response to enable us to react to threats, I am in awe. If you drive a car, for example, you have probably experienced slamming on the brake to avoid hitting another car. Even before you consciously registered an accident was imminent, your foot was already on the brake. It happens very fast – hopefully fast enough to save you (and others) from injury.

So the fight or flight response is perfect for when your survival is threatened.

When your survival is not actually being threatened, though, it's not so perfect. Unfortunately, it does still happen, especially if you have an outdated map. Common situations in which the fight or flight response is unnecessarily engaged might include:

- Public speaking

- Difficult conversations

- First dates

- Speaking with someone you view as important

- Being confronted by another person

- Working to a tight deadline

- A conversation that you consider to be crucial to the achievement of your life goals

Not only is your fight or flight response unnecessary when you're not actually in any physical danger, it's counter-productive. I'm sure you can think of times when you were trying to achieve an outcome, but struggled to be effective because you were shaking or sweating or couldn't think straight.

To respond effectively in difficult situations, such as receiving critical feedback or giving a speech, you need to use the part of your brain that specialises in creativity and problem solving. Creative thinking allows you to respond thoughtfully when your boss gives you critical feedback, identify win/win outcomes in difficult conversations and think on your feet when presenting to a live audience.

If you find you become anxious in these kinds of situations, why not give yourself a reality check. For example:

- Your boss is giving you critical feedback and it feels bad: How likely is it that your boss is going to reach over the table and hit you?

- You have an argument with a close friend and tensions are rising: Do you really think they might physically hurt you or threaten your life?

- You're presenting to an audience and are worried about negative feedback: What are the chances that someone in the audience will leap onto the stage and attack you?

While not impossible, these scenarios are pretty ridiculous, right? Perhaps even comical? Have a laugh at them if you like – having a laugh at yourself helps you get in touch with reality. Isn't it funny that in these kinds of situations, you are responding as if your life's in danger?

Any time you engage your fight or flight response when you're not actually in physical danger, it's a sign that you are navigating your present reality with an outdated map, rather than responding appropriately to what is actually happening.

For example, in the scenario of receiving critical feedback from your boss, let's look at what's going on in your brain and how you might reinterpret the situation more realistically:

> **Scenario:** Your boss is giving you critical feedback. Your brain starts running the following tape: *'What if this is a sign that she is so displeased with my work that she's thinking about firing me? The company has been talking about some cutbacks. If my boss is going to get rid of anyone, it will be the people she isn't happy with, right? What if I don't*

find another job? I really can't afford to lose my job. I could lose my house and become homeless. My life would be over.'

Reality check: If you take a moment to think about this rationally, you probably aren't going to lose your job because of a single piece of feedback. And if you do, you won't likely end up on the street. If you found yourself without a job, it might be upsetting, but you would quickly take action to find another one. It's not losing your job that is your biggest challenge; it's the fear associated with that. As long as your mind even entertains the possibility, it turns an uncomfortable situation into a potentially life-threatening one.

It's important to get in touch with your current reality and recognise that you are not in any physical danger so that you can function from your most effective mindset.

There are no tigers here!

There are various strategies we can use to diffuse the fight or flight response when it is really not necessary. My favourite is incredibly simple. The only reason I don't use it as much as I used to is that my view on what constitutes a life-threatening situation has become more realistic. Still, this strategy comes in handy at those times when I feel the fight or flight response within me.

That is the first step: Notice the physical sensations such as sweating or my heart beating faster and the fearful thoughts.

The second step is to ask myself in a mocking tone, *'Are there any tigers here?'* If that's not enough to bring me back to reality, I continue mocking my fear and say something like, *'Seriously, I don't see any tigers here. Really, I am just talking to another human being. Yes, I want them to like and approve of me, but if they don't, it's highly unlikely that they are going to reach over the table and hit me. I'm not in any danger right now!'*

The mocking tone is important at this point. It diffuses the fear by bringing humour to my irrational behaviour. My brain can then begin to get in touch with reality and register that there is no immediate threat. My body follows, calming down. I feel the calm and, if necessary, remind myself, *'There really is no physical threat right now in this moment.'*

From a place of calm, the part of my brain I need for creativity and problem solving can function optimally – a much better mindset from which to deal with the challenge at hand.

I reiterate, seeing the humorous side is a helpful part of this process. I once had a client, Katherine, report back to me:

"I did the tiger strategy and it didn't work. I noticed myself getting nervous and I told myself, "There's no tiger! There's no tiger!" But I stayed just as panicky and couldn't calm down.""

"Did you do a reality check and have a laugh at yourself for your unnecessary fear response?" I asked.

"No," Katherine responded, "I was more just yelling at myself that there was no tiger."

We were both able to have a chuckle at what she had been doing.

Katherine became very good at the tiger strategy (as it's become known) after that, as did another client who sent me this email:

Hi Kylie,

I was thinking about our Fight or Flight conversation this morning driving to work. I somehow knew I would be taking on a tiger today. It happened around lunch time. I had a vendor I needed to deal with regarding a bad product. Usually I would have an email conversation as it seems to be the easiest way for both of us, but it was going to take too long; I needed to resolve it asap. So instantly I summoned the Tiger strategy. I then made a decision and then called him directly. Long story short, my vendor wanted to take the Flight path and provide me a discount on my next order but I reeled him back in and I received a full refund for the bad product. This might be a small situation for some but it was a WOW moment for me.

Funny ... I had "The eye of the tiger" theme song from Rocky playing in my head after I hung up.

I'm stoked! Thanks Kylie :)
– Dan

It is wonderfully ironic that as soon as you create a 'perception' of safety (even with something as silly as the tiger strategy), you're less likely to need actually need a 'safe' situation, because you're feeling calmer. When you're calm, you're much more able to handle situations that might actually be threatening. But as long as you are thinking, *'Oh no, my boss is going to fire me,'* or *'The audience is going to judge me harshly'*, you're activating your fight or flight response. This, in turn, hinders your ability to think effectively and present well in those situations, making you more likely to create the outcome you most want to avoid. Basically, your brain can't function from the fear centre and the problem-solving centre at the same time, and if your brain ever needs to choose between being creative or keeping you alive, of course, the need to survive will dominate.

By contrast, when you calm yourself, you will quite naturally be able to engage with your pre-frontal cortex, the part of your brain used for decision making, problem solving and creativity. You will feel more confident and others will have more confidence in you, making them more likely to respond favourably to what you say. You will be able to address questions and issues while taking in the whole landscape of the situation and do it from a place of empathy and respect.

Look at all the freedom and the new possibilities and choices that arise from simply understanding more about how your mind works!

Principles of influence

As human beings, we are all susceptible to the principles of influence. Researcher Robert Cialdini identified six influence principles, which are described in his seminal book, *Influence*:[2]

1. **The principle of reciprocation:** We are more likely to give to someone who has previously given to us.

2. **The principle of social proof:** We are more likely to approve of something for which many other people have already given their approval. Similarly, we are more likely to be cautious about something that others have discredited.

3. **The principle of commitment and consistency:** We are more likely to do something if we have committed to it previously, in writing or verbally.

4. **The principle of liking:** We are more likely to say yes to people we already know and like.

5. **The principle of authority:** We are more likely to believe someone in a position of authority.

6. **The principle of scarcity:** We are more likely to want something if we believe there is a limited supply.

Even if these concepts are new to you, you likely recognise intuitively that they have impacted you in the past. With the exception of some cultural differences, these principles have global application. We all tend to give more credence to the opinion of someone wearing a white coat and looks like a doctor. We feel a greater urgency to buy that new jacket if it's the last one available. We're more likely to put faith in a particular product if many of our friends have done the same. And we know that if a friend asks for a favour, we're much more likely to say yes if we feel we owe them one.

None of these things are inherently bad. They can be very helpful and offer practical ways of making effective decisions – as long as the information we are presented with is truthful and ethical.

Unfortunately, we live in a highly commoditised society where much of the information we are faced with throughout the day is positioned to make us buy something. Businesses want us to buy a product or service. During an election, candidates want our votes. Again, there is nothing inherently bad with this, as long as those seeking to influence us are genuine and committed to what is best for us and for the greater good.

However, when making money or gaining power is on another's agenda, your freedom is at risk if you are not aware of your tendency to succumb to the principles of influence. While you might not be aware of them, you can be rest assured most marketers are, and they use these insights constantly to tempt you to buy their products or agree with their policies.

For my client Joanne, a lack of awareness of the principles of influence was getting in the way of her living a life of freedom. Joanne constantly struggled with keeping her finances under control. Simply put, she spent more than she earned. She was having trouble getting her debts resolved, let alone building the wealth portfolio she dreamed about. Joanne was a sucker for new shoes and clothes. Part of the issue was low **self-worth** and thinking that nice things would compensate. The other issue was she was regularly succumbing to the principles of influence. She bought a lot of clothes during sales because they were supposedly cheap and the signs on the shop windows said things like 'hurry, last days' (the principle of scarcity). Joanne wanted to be like a number of the fashion icons and celebrities that she admired, so she purchased the clothes they wore. Joanne also perceived herself as fashionable and had that reputation with her friends, so she wanted to remain consistent with this image (the principle of commitment and consistency).

When Joanne was able to see how the principles of influence were impacting her behaviours, she was able to make adjustments. She was still able to be fashionable but, being much more conscious throughout the process, she started to say "no" to less important purchases. The creation of her wealth portfolio didn't happen overnight but it did become a reality for Joanne, and now she can shop without all the guilt that accompanied her on shopping trips in the past.

Take the time to notice where in your life you might be ineffective or limiting your freedom because you are unknowingly being influenced by the principles.

Being you

Now let's turn our attention to what makes you unique, because there will never be anybody quite like you.

That you have a metaphorical map in your mind makes you human. The content that ends up on your map makes you unique – and that content and the way it plays out in your life involves a combination of your inborn tendencies and your experiences.

Everything you experience in the world, including your sense of freedom, is filtered through your personal lens made up of all your past experiences, influences, values and beliefs. This is both one of the most positive and challenging aspects of being human. Our differences make life so much more interesting and growth-enhancing. However, these differences are also usually the cause of conflicts, whether between two people, communities or nations. So ensuring you understand these differences can help you minimise conflicts, as well as enhance your experience of freedom.

Each of the factors listed below provides a starting point for understanding what makes you unique and why you interpret the world the way you do – it only goes part of the way though, because there is no one theory that will ever fully explain you. As human beings, we are far too complex to be explained by any one theory, so I encourage you to explore how these factors influence you and be open to considering other influences that are uniquely yours.

Your first family

In her book *The Dance of Connection,* Harriet Lerner noted:[3]

> *"Before all else, we are daughters or sons. Our relationships in our first family are the most influential in our lives, and they are never simple."*

There is no escaping the impact of your family, and especially your parents. Even if one or both of your birth parents wasn't around, they still had an impact – sometimes even more so by their absence; just ask someone who's had that experience.

Our parents are usually our greatest source of safety and connection, and also our greatest source of frustration. They care for us and put their hopes, aspirations and fears upon us. They are a major source of our identity, so it's not surprising if we feel we have to rebel against them in order to find ourselves. We can spend an entire lifetime attempting to differentiate between the values our parents instilled in us and the values that are innately ours, and might still struggle to see them clearly at times.

The dynamics of gender and siblings are also powerful influencers of identity. Did you have brothers or sisters or both? And what were your parents' attitudes toward being male or female? Were you the oldest? The youngest? Was there a large age gap between you and the next youngest? Were you an only child? The development of our identities happens at least partly in response to these kinds of dynamics in our families.

There are often patterns in how parents treat children depending on birth order. Many parents joke that they were so cautious with their first born, more relaxed with their second and the third was lucky if they got any attention at all! Jokes aside, it makes sense that parents become more relaxed in their parenting as they gain more skills and experience. These commonly-seen patterns in parenting styles have produced a theory of birth order which suggests that:

- First born children tend to be reliable, conscientious, structured, cautious and high achievers;

- Middle children tend to be people pleasers, peace-makers, independent and strong negotiators;

- Youngest children tend to be fun-loving, uncomplicated, manipulative, competitive and attention seeking; and

- Only children tend to be mature, leaders, selfish, strong achievers and typically have high self-esteem.

Family dynamics gains another layer of complexity when you factor in gender. For example, a middle child of all girls will likely have a very different experience from a female middle child between two boys. And some parents have been known to place the responsibilities of an oldest child on their son, even if he has an older sister, if they believe those responsibilities should belong to a male.

All the above suggestions are tendencies, not certainties; there are always exceptions and no one theory can explain why your personality developed the way it did. What is certain is that, regardless of how rigid or relaxed your parents were, no matter your gender or where you sat in the family, your experiences created both strengths and weaknesses and contributed numerous rules to your map. Your personal freedom will be enhanced by understanding these strengths and weakness, recognising how they developed and making conscious decisions about whether to accept or rewrite your rules to suit your current and future circumstances.

The more conscious you are about your map and your ability to explore and update it over time, the greater your experience of freedom.

Culture

You are influenced by the culture in which you live.

We all know the messages about how we should behave and the judgements put upon us according to our age, gender, religion or race. There are expectations about whether you should be married and to whom, about how feminine or masculine you should or shouldn't be, and about how many children you should have. There are expectations about whether you should or shouldn't work if you have children, about whether children should be breastfed and where that breastfeeding should occur. There are expectations about what you should wear, what opinions you should have, what you should eat and how much you should weigh. These and many other expectations are usually a reflection of the culture in which you live and serve as powerful reinforcers, often leaving us battling between the expectations others have of us and what we want for ourselves.

The impact of your culture can be reinforced, diluted or completely rejected by the family in which you were raised. For example, cultures in most countries tend to dictate that men are more valuable in the workplace than women, as is evidenced by well-documented pay disparities between men and women for similar roles. Your first family may be one that assimilates with these expectations of men and women. Or your family may promote equality through their words and actions, leading you to feel more inclined to disregard such cultural expectations. To varying degrees, individual families tend to align with the culture within which they exist.

Ziauddin Yousafzai, the father of Pakistani human rights activist Malala Yousafzai, had aspirations for his family that went against the expectations of their local culture. In a presentation, Yousafzai explained that in Pakistan's patriarchal society, the birth of a girl is not celebrated and is often not even welcomed by her parents. When she is five, she stays at home while her brothers go to school. If she is to be considered a good girl, she should be very quiet, humble and submissive.

Yousafzai wanted something different for his daughter. He felt the norms of his society went against the basic human rights of women and discriminatory laws needed to be abolished. He enrolled Malala into school and taught her to unlearn the lesson of constant obedience. These lessons were not lost on Malala, who had a hunger for education, and by the age of ten, had captured media attention worldwide by taking a public stand for the right of girls to an education.

Unfortunately, extremists would not tolerate Malala's campaign and in October 2012, she was shot in the head at point blank range. This was devastating for Malala's parents and her father wondered whether he was to blame for this tragic event. Yousafzai's wife said he should not blame himself, for he and Malala stood for the right cause - the cause of education.

Fortunately for humanity, Malala and her fighting spirit survived and in October 2014 she became the youngest person ever to receive a Nobel Prize. When Ziauddin Yousafzai was asked what he taught his daughter that encouraged her to be so courageous, he said it was not so much what he did, but rather what he didn't do: he did not clip her wings. He made it sound like a simple thing, but when viewed through the context of culture, it was truly impressive.

We can learn from Yousafzai's story. We can see the impact that culture can have on our family and, in turn, on ourselves. While it is fortunate that most of us in Western countries are unlikely to end up in life-threatening situations if we take a stand against our cultural dictates, it is still the case that culture exerts a powerful influence on who we become and how we view the world.

Creating self-knowledge

To create freedom, you first need to see where you are not free. Let's look at how you can broaden your knowledge of who you are and why you behave the way you do, including where these behaviours are limiting your freedom. The following sections are designed to help you tap into these insights about yourself.

Get curious and ask questions

Curiosity is a fundamental requirement for enhancing self-knowledge.

Curiosity will help you discover and appreciate both your strengths and areas for improvement and how they impact your experience of freedom.

The questions below can help get you started. Ask yourself a question and then trust whatever comes to mind in response. None of your responses need to be viewed as positive or negative. They are simply insights to understand yourself and why you experience the world the way you do. Your responses can highlight where you might be preventing your own freedom. You could explore the questions on your own or with a friend, and write your responses in your journal.

- What do I like about myself? Why? What's happened in my life that makes me think that way?

- What don't I like about myself? What has influence my opinion?

- What am I afraid of? How do I respond when I'm afraid? What would I do if I wasn't afraid?

- What do I think about other people in my life? Why do I think that?

- What are my strengths? Where do they help me and when do they become a problem?

- What are my weaknesses? How have my weaknesses served me?

- What stops me from speaking my truth? How does that benefit or constrain me?

Exploring questions such as these can take time but it is well worth the effort. If time is limited, it might be more valuable to go deep with just a few rather than attempt to answer all of them superficially.

These questions are designed to provide insight about what you think, how those thoughts connect to your experiences of not being free and what you need to be aware of to change. This is why your own mind sometimes has a tendency to resist answering them. Part of you craves safety, wanting things to be the same and predictable, and resists both change and progress. But creating freedom often means making changes.

The resistance can be subtle and sly, so watch out for it. In coaching sessions, I frequently ask questions that don't get answered (not at first, anyway). One of the most common examples is when I ask, "What do you want?" Very often, my client will respond by explaining what they don't want, rather than what they do. Most of us actually don't know what we want for ourselves because, even if we ask the question, we don't take the time to answer it properly. Another example of resistance is when I ask a question and my client avoids giving a direct response. As they continue talking, it's clear to me that they haven't answered the question, but my client is often completely unaware. This resistance is quite human and normal. I just wait for them to finish their sentence and then respectfully ask the question again.

If you're experiencing resistance when exploring these questions, you will likely find value in having a friend or coach explore them with you and hold you accountable when it comes to providing responses.

Pay attention to what triggers you

You can learn a great deal about yourself by paying attention to what triggers you.

Sometimes triggers cause positive responses, like when you see your child at the end of the school day. As soon as they see you too, their face lights up with recognition and a smile that lets you know how happy they are to see you. This trigger (seeing your child happy) has caused your whole body to respond positively, making you feel great. Or imagine the physical response that occurs if you notice a loved one is being threatened in some way. It's an instant change in your body.

What are these positive or negative changes about? They are reflections of your most powerful and deeply ingrained beliefs, values, desires and fears – all of which are located on your map somewhere and have been triggered by something that you experienced in your world.

I know several people who were bitten by dogs when they were children. All except one continue to be triggered, sometimes severely, whenever they encounter a dog or even think about being near a dog. The one person who rarely gets triggered anymore said she had done a lot of work on herself, including with a therapist, to understand the connections she had made between the dog that attacked her and all dogs. Now, the only times she has a negative response to a dog, it is not unreasonable. She still feels that if she were to encounter a large, hostile looking dog, she would be very concerned, but this is a normal response for most people.

Take notice of when you are triggered and be curious. Sometimes the causes of your triggers are not as obvious as the connection between being attacked by a dog and a fear of dogs. For example, one client noticed that she was consistently triggered when her husband was late arriving home, even if it was only a short time after he was due. She would remain on high alert until she knew where he was. She tried to manage this situation by using guilt to manipulate her husband and ensure he was never even a minute late without providing regular updates on his whereabouts. With a willingness to explore, she recognised that her husband's lateness triggered childhood memories of feeling abandoned by her father. By clarifying the trigger and understanding her response, she was able to begin the work of updating her map so that it would be more relevant to a grown woman.

Clarity is power. The more clarity you have about what triggers you, the more powerfully you can respond in the future. Doesn't that sound like freedom?

Look within to understand your world without

My friend Carina shared a very powerful story about how she learned self-respect. For a couple of years, she had been feeling disrespected by her daughter. It really upset and angered Carina and she let her daughter know. Sometimes her daughter apologised; sometimes she didn't. Either way, Carina didn't really feel much changed and continued to feel disrespected. Then Carina learned about projection and how what we experience in others is always, even if we can't see it, a reflection of what occurs within us. With this new understanding, Carina stopped judging her daughter's disrespect and instead began asking, *'Where am I not respecting myself?'* Immediately, she could see ways she was not respecting herself.

Like Carina, we can also gain powerful insights when we choose to look at what we are projecting outwards as an indication of what we experience within.

Notice if you criticise your partner for not being loving towards you. Do you treat yourself with love? Do you dedicate enough time to self-care? Do you feel you are unlovable and unknowingly expect your partner to compensate for this feeling?

Notice if you are regularly judging people for their weight. Do you also criticise yourself for your weight? Do you criticise yourself for not doing enough exercise? Are you prone to emotional eating?

Notice if you criticise anyone who hasn't completed a task to your standard. Do you believe that you need to do things perfectly? Do you ever lie about how well you have completed a task? Were you regularly judged for not being good enough in the past?

Notice if you are judgemental about the way someone chooses to spend their money. Do you tell yourself that you are terrible at managing your finances? Do you ever deprive yourself of something you want even if you can afford it? Do you have a scarcity mentality?

The above are just a few examples of how you can turn your judgements around to gain greater knowledge about yourself. With these powerful insights, you can then choose to put **energy** into changing the things you notice about yourself rather than judging others. This is exactly what Carina did. She stopped complaining about her daughter and instead began treating herself with respect. Carina said, like magic, her daughter began being more respectful of her too.

We teach people how to treat us. You can take **responsibility** for changing these situations, but you first need to be able to see the core issue.

"Everything that irritates us about others can lead us to an understanding of ourselves."

– Carl Jung

Understand you are always evolving

It is important, during your explorations, not to get too attached to a particular outcome. You are always developing and evolving.

If you are too judgemental in the process of your explorations, you risk missing out on key insights. And if you are too attached to needing your 'self' to appear a particular way, you might miss the truth about who you are really being.

There is no end point in your journey to self-knowledge. So you are free to enjoy the journey of gathering insights and learning, without worrying about reaching some final goal.

Keep this in mind any time you are feeling uncertain about your own identity, or if an identity you choose for yourself clashes with the expectations that others have of you. You are always an extraordinary work in progress.

I have worked with clients who made big changes in their career plans because the work they thought they wanted to do turned out to be something they really disliked or no longer valued. I've also worked with clients who, after a long-term relationship a man, chose to be in a relationship with a woman. In these cases and others like them, the person usually needs some time to adjust. Where they once might have felt certain about who they were, their future is now more fluid and less predictable. This can be both exciting and scary as they explore new possibilities for their life.

Evolving doesn't mean you need to spend every moment in reflection, but any time you do invest in self-exploration reaps immeasurable benefits.

"The unexamined life is not worth living."

– Socrates

Chapter summary

- Self-knowledge is the first key to unlocking your freedom.

- To enhance self-knowledge, you can engage in honest self-exploration and commit to examining both the positive and negative aspects of how you are being, including where you have room to improve.

- Our society suffers from an epidemic of self-deception. Most of us learnt to hide parts of ourselves from others and even ourselves.

- Understanding some of the universal truths about being human can help you understand why you do the things you do and how to live your most authentic life.

- Everyone has a metaphorical map inside their head they use to navigate the world. While this map functions well if relevant to our environment, it can get us into trouble if it becomes outdated and no longer relevant to our current life situation.

- An outdated map might cause you to engage your fight or flight response when you are not in any real physical danger. This can prevent you from experiencing true freedom in life if you then try to avoid those situations.

- It is possible to rewrite the map in your head and create one that serves you better, moving you in the direction you want to go.

- Being aware of the principles of influence can assist you in ensuring they are not causing you to be ineffective and limiting your freedom.

- Your family has a powerful influence in shaping how you view the world.

- Every life experience contributes to your uniqueness.

- Culture has a powerful influence on how you experience the world.

- You can enhance self-knowledge by answering exploratory questions, ensuring you answer honestly, even if it means getting a friend or coach to assist you. You can also pay attention to what triggers you and how you judge others, as this is usually a reflection of how you view yourself.

- You are always in development and always evolving. You don't need to spend every moment of your life in reflection, but any time you do invest reaps immeasurable benefits.

You literally become a different person when you change your thoughts and change the meanings you attach to what happens.

ELEMENT 2:

MEANING

Carla had an appointment for laser eye surgery scheduled with an eye specialist six weeks in advance. Eager to be free of wearing glasses, she felt frustrated when, a week before her appointment, the clinic called to let her know that her doctor would be overseas longer than expected. The clinic asked Carla to push her appointment back two weeks.

Begrudgingly, Carla agreed, all the while imagining her doctor at some extravagant holiday resort. *'Who does she think she is?'* Carla thought. *'Does she think she can just extend holidays whenever she likes, causing patients to adjust all the plans they've had in place for weeks? Perhaps she should try living in the real world like the rest of us.'*

Over the next few weeks, every time Carla thought of her doctor, she felt the tension of resentment. Several times, she almost cancelled her appointment because she thought she would be more suited to a doctor with a better work ethic. So Carla was quite surprised when the time came for her appointment and the doctor walked in and began apologising. "I'm very sorry that we had to reschedule your appointment. I was doing volunteer work at a village in Africa, working in partnership with local doctors to restore sight to the children who live there. It wasn't until after I arrived that I learned there were more children to treat than expected."

In that moment, Carla's reality changed. Nothing external had changed, only the meaning she attached to the situation. She no longer had any negative feelings towards her doctor; it was quite the contrary. Now it seemed obvious that her doctor must not only be a highly talented eye specialist, but a wonderful human being as well.

We attach meaning to everything

Human beings attach meaning to everything. It's something our brains need to do so that we can function in the world and make sense of everything we encounter. Even when we say that something means nothing, we created meaning.

Furthermore, we usually treat the meanings we have created like empirical evidence we have gathered based on extensive research that is one hundred per cent accurate. Then, because we're so certain that we're right, we act and feel in ways that align with the story that we made up. This is a problem because our created meanings rarely equal reality.

In Carla's case, her initial interpretation of her doctor's actions was very negative. This caused her to feel unnecessary stress and resentment, and almost resulted in cancelling her appointment and wait even longer for surgery with another doctor. In reality, Carla's doctor was attempting to do right. When Carla realised, her experience of the situation and the meaning she gave it changed.

I did a similar thing to Carla while I was writing this book. Less than a week before my book was due for second round edits, my father called to say that he, my mother and my two nephews were going to be in town for the weekend. While he was probably expecting me to be happy about that news, I got upset with him. I thought, *'Why are they visiting while I'm on a writing deadline? Why couldn't he have picked a weekend when I was free to spend time with them? Why did they tell me with one day's notice? If he had given me more warning, I could have negotiated a different due date with my editor.'*

In my frustration, I also added the following meanings: *'He doesn't care enough to check in with me before making plans and then just expects me to be available. He only cares about what's convenient for him and then expects me to just drop everything and fit in with their plans.'*

The reality, of course, is that my father cares about me deeply. His plans were a last-minute idea and it needed to be that weekend because it would be the last opportunity before my nephews went back to school. I was nearing the end of a long period of writing, which was sometimes a lonely task, and in that moment I was feeling mentally exhausted – none of which had anything to do with my father.

Yet in the moment, I was so frustrated that, instead of sharing in his excitement that we would be spending time together, I added meanings that were not true and that upset me. I left the phone conversation feeling disappointed.

How often do you do this? Think of all the times someone you care about has done something that upset you, and you made it mean they don't care. Just as in my example, what is more likely is they just happened to do something without realising how it might affect you. You were the one who made it mean they don't care and it was this meaning rather than their actions that upset you.

Perhaps the other person could have been more empathetic about your situation. But if they weren't, it's rarely because they don't care, especially if it's someone close to you. Some people do not empathise well. It doesn't mean they don't care. Most people care, but they don't always show it in the way we want.

It could have been the case that Carla's doctor was selfish. People do behave selfishly sometimes. But do you really want to make that your first judgement of someone when you have no evidence to support your claims? Until such time that you can confirm the reality of the situation, your judgements do nothing to the other person, but they do make you miserable.

The question is, do you want to be miserable (and possibly right), or do you want to be happy and free? Do you want to be free from the need to control what other people do? Do you want to be free from the need to have other people behave a certain way before you can go out and live your life the way you want to?

Of course, you want to be free. And experiencing freedom means taking **responsibility** for the meanings we create.

From a place of awareness of and responsibility for the meanings I created, I called my father. I apologised for getting upset, acknowledging my reaction was much more about what was already going on in my own life than a reaction to what he did. In that moment, not much in the external world had changed, but I felt free – free from the pain, free from being a victim of life circumstances and free to create options and ways to spend time with family and get my book finished.

"There are no facts, only interpretations."

– Friedrich Nietzsche

"Changing your perception of the world is often as good as changing the world— but it also allows a person to be miserable even when all the material and social conditions for happiness have been met. During the normal course of events, your mind will determine the quality of your life."

– Sam Harris

You are the creator of meanings and miracles

You are the creator of meaning. This means you have the power to *choose* how you perceive and experience everything in your life. You choose how you experience people, regardless of what they do. You choose your perspective on an event. It's all within your power.

Many people struggle with this concept, especially when they are new to it. I still have to remind myself regularly.

But this is an important one to understand and one of the most valuable skills you will ever learn.

Wise people do not underestimate the potential value of a shift in perspective or the impact of the meanings they create.

A shift in perspective can end a war.

A shift in perspective can stop the human race from destroying the planet.

A shift in perspective can put food in the mouth of every starving child.

A shift in perspective can create your freedom.

Considering all that it can create, a shift in perspective is more than just changing your mind or seeing something new – it's a miracle.

Wouldn't it be miraculous if we humans removed the perspective of fear that so pervades our world?

Would not a world of possibilities open up if we shifted our perspectives from fear to curiosity?

Wouldn't it be a revelation to see every person, including yourself, for who they really are? To understand others and to be understood?

This doesn't have to be a fantasy. Living a life of freedom doesn't have to be some far-off dream. You have the power to create it because you are the creator of meaning.

> *"Could a greater miracle take place than*
> *for us to look through each other's eyes for*
> *an instant?"*
>
> **– Henry David Thoreau**

Developing the element of meaning

Your freedom lies in how well you create empowering meanings. Over the following pages, I will discuss five ways to do just that:

1. Don't believe everything you think.

2. Choose the story that makes you feel better.

3. Recognise that everyone is calling for love.

4. Ask four powerful questions.

5. Forge meaning.

Then I'll share with you a list of my most often used freedom thoughts – I use them any time that I am feeling stuck or my life is not working. They never fail to remind me that I have power over the meanings that I create and give me a more empowered and liberated perspective.

> *"Life is without meaning. You bring the meaning to it. The meaning of life is whatever you ascribe it to be."*
>
> **– Joseph Campbell**

Don't believe everything you think

When I look back on my life fifteen years ago, I think, *'Wow, I really didn't know anything back then.'*

I don't mean that literally. I had a tertiary education and I'd travelled across five continents. I'd learned many things, had lots of life experiences and taken advantage of many opportunities. And yet, I still look back at the person I was and many of the beliefs I held and think that I really didn't know much.

Ironically, one of the key differences between who I was then and who I am now is that, back then, I thought I knew it all. It's very likely in fifteen years, I'll look back to this year and realise how little I knew still. It's humbling and it frees me from needing to know everything.

There is so much power in realising the beliefs I carried around for so long existed simply because of the environments I'd experienced. If I'd grown up in a Catholic family with religious traditions then I probably would have developed a set of beliefs in accordance with that experience. The same would be true if I'd grown up in a Jewish, Muslim or a politically-oriented family. If I grew up in different century, I might have believed it was my proper role to have children, live to serve my husband and disregard any notions of getting an education.

The beliefs on which you were raised are your guides, but they are often your blinders too.

Freedom exists in a flexible mind and the ability to create your own meanings rather than those ascribed to you.

Ask yourself questions about the beliefs you hold. Here are just some examples:

- What do I believe about myself?

- What do I believe about the people in my life?

- What do I believe is likely to happen in the future?

- What do I believe about money?

- What do I believe about following the call of my spirit?

Once you've named your beliefs, ask yourself: Do these beliefs empower me and enhance my freedom?

If your beliefs don't enhance your freedom, do you need them? Would you be willing to let those beliefs go if it meant you could experience more freedom?

Then, from a place of **courage**, ask:

- If I let go of fear, what empowering beliefs would I choose for myself?

Take the time to dig deep. You may find it easier if you do the exercise with a friend. Ask each other these questions and be willing to hold each other accountable and take **responsibility** for the meanings and beliefs to which you adhere.

> *"The well-bred contradict other people. The wise contradict themselves."*
>
> **– Oscar Wilde**

Don't believe everything you think, especially if what you think and the meanings you created are hindering your sense of personal freedom, or creating distance and hurt rather than connection and love. You have already experienced enough in your life to know that what you once believed can later prove to be false, and what was once unimaginable or seemed impossible can become 'normal'.

Choose the story that makes you feel better

A second approach to adopting meanings that enhance your freedom is to choose the story which makes you feel better.

This may sound simplistic, but life really doesn't need to be more complex than this.

If we return to Carla from the beginning of this chapter, her original interpretation of her doctor's overseas trip was very judgmental and her story did not make her feel good. She could have chosen a different story rather than one making her feel resentful. It might have been that her doctor was learning a cutting-edge technique to improve her skills (and Carla's surgery as a result), or she could have been taking some much needed time off so she would perform at her best when she worked on Carla's eyes. These are just stories, but either would have made Carla feel better than just assuming that her doctor didn't care enough about her clients or take her responsibilities seriously.

This is not about being naïvely optimistic. If Carla found out for a fact that her doctor was irresponsible then it would have been wise to make alternative arrangements for the surgery. Until such time that Carla had those facts, however, she could free herself from the misery caused by her unfounded negative stories.

This is about letting go of unnecessary cynicism. I've encountered a lot of cynics. They live in the reality that their cynicism (often applied to people they don't know and situations they know little about) is justified because they encounter so much poor behaviour in the world around them. In my view, these people contribute to the world's negativity. They have an outdated map that keeps them hypersensitive to poor behaviour. This is not freedom; rather, it is a perspective that keeps them small and separated from others.

Until you have the facts, keep an open mind. Set yourself free. Choose the story that makes you feel better.

To assist with living by this philosophy, keep these three points in mind:

- Feeling better is not achieved by making others feel worse. Your spirit knows that how you treat others is how you treat yourself. If you feel better when you have judged or put down another, you are more connected to your ego than your spirit. The good feeling in that instance doesn't last (if it ever feels good at all).

- Choosing a story that makes you feel better is not being naïve. If your partner has an affair, feeling better might mean forgiving them, but it doesn't have to mean staying with that person. If your child has a substance addiction, feeling better might mean continuing to love them and being supportive if they want to recover, but it doesn't mean putting up with abuse.

- Feeling better does not necessarily mean you will feel happy. For instance, feeling better sometimes means allowing yourself to feel sad or to feel the discomfort that might come from saying 'no' to someone you care about or to spend time discussing uncomfortable topics with a therapist. Feeling better through alignment with your spirit will, however, lead to contentment or peace in the long term, even if it does not bring you joy in the short term.

Choosing the story that makes you feel better puts you back in control. It is a way of taking **responsibility** and it frees you from being a victim of your circumstances.

"If you get up in the morning and think the future is going to be better, it is a bright day. Otherwise, it's not."

– Elon Musk

"Your whole perspective on the world will shift by just a little, every time you let your mind escape its chains."

– A Course in Miracles

Recognise everyone's call for love

Every time someone (you and me included) does something to offend or hurt another, whether they realise it or not, it's very likely they are attempting to make themselves feel better in some way.

Everyone is fighting their own battle. When we remember this, it is easier to be kind – to others and ourselves. Often we forget. Often we feel alone. Often we have outdated maps in our minds and a history of feeling wrong or not good enough. It's not surprising that most people experience underlying, sometimes overt, fear and unhappiness. It can lead people to do things that offend, hurt or anger others.

This underlying fear and unhappiness is sometimes the only explanation I can find for the way people treat each other when they are being hurtful, offensive or violent – be it physical, verbal or emotional. Wounded people feel the need to wound others.

But if you listen carefully, or read between the lines of some of the hurt or hate-filled words and behaviours, you can hear it and see it. People are saying: Love me.

Some variants are 'respect me' or 'look after me' or 'help me' or 'be proud of me' or 'adore me' or 'listen to me' or 'understand me'. But underneath each one is the same call for love and understanding.

We often forget this because we get caught up in our own lives, our own battles. We get distracted by what we see on the surface. But we can choose to remember and we can choose to add the meaning: They are asking for love.

How would you respond to others if you saw their words and actions as a call for love?

Perhaps you could make this interpretation:

> *Their actions are not even about me. They hurt others because they are hurting. I could choose peace instead of making it mean that they intend to hurt me. I could set myself free instead of engaging with their negativity.*

This is not about saying, 'It's fine that you treated me so badly. I'll put up with it.' Sometimes, the loving thing to do is say "no". Sometimes the loving thing to do is leave. Both of these can be done while remembering that everyone is asking for love in the ways they know how. Remembering this will position you to respond to the unnecessarily damaging actions of others with clarity and composure, both of which will have you feeling better about yourself, not worse.

Like choosing the story that makes you feel better, recognising everyone's call for love is not about being naïve. There is evil in the world and we do need to be vigilant about eradicating such evils.

However, overcoming the evil in the world starts with managing the perceived evils in our own lives rather than just defaulting to fear.

What happens when you respond to fear with fear? What good comes of that?

If you're a scary person, perhaps others will submit to your demands. However, the result is submission, not the love you ultimately crave. You may gain a perception of safety because you overpowered them, but you will not experience spiritual growth.

In your everyday life, you are dealing with people just like you. These people could include your partner, children, the mother or father of your children, your parents, closest friends, colleagues and even strangers. They are all human beings who are trying their best to make their way through life the only way they know how – just like you.

So why do so many of us behave as though we are surrounded by criminals who wronged us and who need to be judged and punished for the crimes we feel were committed against us?

When we judge in this way, we are *encouraging* the very behaviour that offends us.

People are less likely to behave at their best when you express concerns about their flaws and imminent failure. Unless the other person is more aware than you about their thoughts and behaviours, and chooses to respond positively in spite of your negativity, they'll probably react in a similarly insecure way. The next thing you know, you have two insecure people arguing and both are more likely to create the thing they fear most.

Think for a moment about all of the time you spend being critical of others because they haven't behaved in the way you think they should. Think about all the mental **energy** you put into devising plans for how you can gather evidence of their bad behaviour or making them behave differently.

Many of these people who you put on trial for perceived crimes in the courthouse of your mind are probably people you claim to love. Yet love doesn't force another to change – love accepts and communicates and seeks to understand.

You know this because you've felt the hurt of being judged by those you love and want to believe love you. You know that you feel most loved by another person when they appreciate you for all that you do and for all that you are, just the way you are.

If someone behaves poorly, while you don't need to condone their behaviour, you can remind yourself before you respond that they, like you, are seeking love and attempting in their own way to make themselves feel better.

> *"All the evidence that we have indicates that it is reasonable to assume in practically every human being, and certainly in almost every newborn baby, that there is an active will toward health, an impulse toward growth, or toward the actualisation of human potentialities."*
>
> **– Abraham Maslow**

Ask four powerful questions

Every feeling is preceded by a thought.

Every behaviour is preceded by a thought.

Therefore, if you want to change your feelings or your behaviours, you need to change your thoughts.

Four of the most power questions I ever learned that assist with exploring and understanding the thoughts and meanings I create, and how they impact my feelings and behaviours, I learned from Byron Katie's book *Loving What Is*.[4] These four questions rarely fail to give me clarity about the meanings I create and how they impact my behaviour. These four questions are:

1. Is it true?

2. Can you absolutely know that it's true?

3. How do you react when you think that thought?

4. Who would you be without that thought?

You can use these four questions any time you are experiencing some kind of upset.

Pick any of the thoughts that lie beneath the feeling and apply the four questions.

For example, let's imagine that when you look beneath negative feelings, you find the thought '*I'm not good enough.*' Let's imagine the context is that you want someone in your life to be impressed with you but you don't feel they are; perhaps it's your spouse, your boss or your child. One of the meanings that you applied to their lack of enthusiasm is that you're not good enough.

Now that you've narrowed in on the thought beneath your feelings and behaviours, let's explore the thought '*I'm not good enough*' with the four questions.

Is it true? You know it's not. Or perhaps you tell yourself its not, but you have doubts. Either way, the second question will always help you find the answer if the first one doesn't …

Can you absolutely know that it's true? No. You can't absolutely know anything for sure. Ever. Nothing is black and white. Even in the unlikely circumstance that the other person actually says the words "You're not good enough," it doesn't mean it's true. Of course it doesn't. Nobody could ever make that decision except you.

What's even more important than whether it's true is how it makes you feel and how you behave as a result of that thought.

How do you react when you have that thought? When I ask this question of clients, common responses are: "I get frustrated," "I behave passive aggressively," "I avoid them," "I get angry at them," and "I get depressed," to name a few. It makes sense – these are quite logical and typical responses for any human being to the thought '*I'm not good enough.*'

Who would you be without that thought? Common responses to this question are: "I'd be getting on with my life," "I would tell them how I feel," "I'd be happy." This question is so much more powerful than simply asking, "What would you do?" It's about who you would *be*. You literally become a different person when you change your thoughts and change the meanings you attach to what happens.

My most common response to the last question is: I'd be free.

These four questions are so effective; they can be applied to even the most challenging situations. I had a powerful realisation the day I applied these questions to the pain I felt at the loss of someone I loved. The thought that kept bringing me pain was, '*They shouldn't have died.*' I struggled with the second question – I really believed they shouldn't have died. But we can never know anything for sure. We don't know what might lie ahead as a result of what happened in the past. Instead, I could realise that one thought, that one fight against reality, was keeping me in pain. As long as I had that thought, I was stuck. I did not move on. When I found the **courage** to explore who I would be without that thought, I was free to accept, free to grieve and free to begin creating a life that the person I loved would be proud of.

The list of meanings and thoughts we create that keep us stuck is endless ... 'He shouldn't have cheated on me.' 'They shouldn't have fired me.' 'There shouldn't be any terrorism.' 'She did it on purpose.' 'He was trying to hurt me.' 'No matter what I do, I always lose.' 'My father let me down.' 'I failed.' And so on.

But we can never know anything for sure. So how does holding onto negative meanings serve you? How does it serve the world? Let go of those thoughts and allow yourself to be the person you could be if you freed yourself from those thoughts.

> *"Life just happens. It's what you're believing about life that makes you suffer."*
>
> – Byron Katie

Forge meaning

It should be easy to change disempowering meanings to ones that enhance freedom. You just change your mind, right? Or as we've discussed, you simply choose the story that makes you feel better. You could choose to believe that everything in your life has happened for a reason that ultimately serves you and moves you forward, trusting that the reason will eventually be revealed. Sometimes it is that easy.

Other times it's more difficult. Some life experiences leave us feeling challenged in ways we've never dealt with before. We may fall, literally or metaphorically, to our knees, completely unsure about what to do next. At times like these, it often doesn't help to trivialise our challenges. Our pain is real. Our devastation is real. Our heartbreak is real. Rising above such challenging experiences in order to find a meaning that sets us free might be as simple as a change in perspective, but it can sometimes take an incredible amount of mental and emotional strength to do so.

In his TED talk, Andrew Solomon describes how moving forward powerfully in the wake of tragedies and challenges is not done by simply finding meaning, but by *forging* meaning.[5]

Forging meaning is the concerted effort that you make day after day after day to create empowering meanings. You should never underestimate the effort this sometimes requires, particularly when you are experiencing heartache, defeat or despair. It always takes **courage** to keep moving into an unknown future, and this is never more true than after you faced a challenge – when the self that you were and the life you once knew have been irrevocably changed.

Solomon researched how some families manage to deal with having challenging or unusual children and how they find meaning in spite of their challenges. A mother with two children with multiple severe disabilities recounted, "People always give us these little sayings like, "God doesn't give you any more than you can handle," but children like ours are not preordained as a gift. They're a gift because that's what we have chosen." In other words, in spite of the difficulties, this mother *chose* to see her children as a gift – she forged a new meaning that served her and her children.

Sometimes this concerted effort is all you can do, and your best chance of finding the gift in your challenges. "Such a gift," explains Solomon, "does not make what was wrong right; it only makes what was wrong precious."

This power over meaning exists in all of us, in spite of challenges and self-doubts. In his book *Man's Search for Meaning*, Victor Frankl recognised that it's difficult to create meaning for our lives in trying times. This is something he knew all too well through observing himself and those around him while incarcerated in a concentration camp. During this time, he witnessed people creating empowering meanings in spite of all they had suffered and he believed if it was possible for them, it proved that anyone can rise above their own fate.[6]

So always look for a meaning that serves and empowers you. Even when it is something you need to forge with whatever strength you can muster in the wake of challenging times. Life's trials do not last forever and, at a minimum, what those challenges mean is you can not only survive, but you can also take what you have learned and create an even stronger and wiser self.

> *"If you're going through hell, keep going."*
>
> **– Winston Churchill**

Freedom thoughts (author's favourites)

Below is a list of quotes or sayings I've picked up throughout my life that I use regularly to remind myself that I am in charge of the meanings I create and to assist me in creating more empowering meanings when necessary. I call them 'freedom thoughts' because reminding myself of them always creates a greater sense of freedom. Whenever I encounter challenges, I usually find myself repeating whichever one is most appropriate. I continue to use them because they work.

Sometimes the reminder is all I need to just let go of whatever the challenge is, or let go of the perception that it is even a challenge, or position myself to handle life more effectively. At a minimum, the reminder always seems to make life easier. I've been reminding myself of these freedom thoughts for such a long time now that, these days, they come to mind naturally when needed, but it wasn't always so natural. If they feel new to you and you think they could be useful, I suggest keeping a copy of them where you will be reminded in times of challenge.

'Life is difficult.'

This is the first line in *The Road Less Travelled* by M. Scott Peck[7]. Peck follows that line with, "This is a great truth, one of the greatest truths. It is a great truth because once we truly see this truth, we transcend it. Once we truly know that life is difficult – once we truly understand and accept it – then life is no longer difficult. Because once it is accepted, the fact that life is difficult no longer matters."

These words work on me like magic. What was difficult – life – is suddenly no longer difficult because I'm no longer fighting against a belief that 'life should be easy'. Instead, I just accept that life is difficult and turn my attention to thinking about the best way to live it and handle its inevitable challenges.

'Whenever I fight with reality, I always lose.'

Like the four questions discussed earlier in this chapter, I learned this one from Byron Katie. Reality is what reality is. There are some things I can change and there are some things I can't. I can't change that people get old and die. I can't turn back time in the wake of a tragedy. I can't force someone to love me, or even respect me. If I find myself getting frustrated about anything I can't change, I'm in a fight with reality and that's a fight I can't win. This reminder helps me to let go and frees me to put my energy into those things I can influence.

'The normal people are the ones you don't know very well.'

This is a great reminder any time I am comparing myself to others, especially if I'm adding meanings about how there is something wrong with me or my life, while everyone else is living the happy life. Even though I know creating meanings like that is nonsensical, sometimes I forget. So this saying reminds me there are no 'normal' people. Everybody has challenges, family secrets and things they feel weird about. That's the truth. In thousands of hours of coaching, I've heard clients share so many secrets that they think make them weird or faulty. I am no weirder than anyone else and that, by definition, means I'm not weird. But sometimes in the middle of a challenging week, I can find myself comparing the behind-the-scenes aspects of my life to someone else's highlight reel. I often feel weird, but this quote, and the friends and clients I know well, help remind me that I'm not alone.

'Celebrate the haters.'

When my friend and I decided we would create a podcast for busy professionals who want to thrive, we also made an agreement that we were going to celebrate our first 'hater'. The haters are people who don't like what you do and feel the need to tell you – and they are inevitable if you are putting your opinions out for public consumption. We wanted to stay committed to speaking our minds and being our most authentic selves on the show, so we decided that the first hater would be something to celebrate rather than fear, because the first hater would be recognition that we are expressing our minds authentically rather than attempting to please everyone.

'If I chose for this to happen for a positive reason, what would that be?'

This question encourages me to search for the positive when I'm struggling to see one. Sometimes the positive is more empathy for others experiencing similar challenges. Sometimes it's uncovering strength I didn't know I had. At a minimum, I am usually reminded that my challenges teach me the lessons that will serve me in the future.

> *"You live, you learn. You love, you learn. You cry, you learn. You lose, you learn. You bleed, you learn."*
>
> **– Alanis Morissette**

Chapter summary

- As human beings, we attach meaning to everything. There is no single truth or reality – there is only interpretation and created meanings.

- The meanings you create determine your feelings and behaviours. These then create your life, including the degree of freedom you experience.

- If you want to change your feelings or your behaviours, you need to change your thoughts.

- Wise people do not underestimate the potential value of a shift in perspective or the impact of the meanings they create.

- Choosing the meaning that serves you is a way of taking **responsibility** and frees you from being a victim of your circumstances.

- Understanding that everyone is yearning for love can help you interpret events in a more charitable light, rather than simply passing judgement.

- Choosing stories that make you feel better can free you from the disempowerment associated with negative meanings.

- Finding a meaning that enhances your freedom can be difficult. Sometimes it's not so much that you *find* meaning, but *forge* meaning, in order to create freedom and greater happiness.

- Creating a deeper sense of meaning or purpose can help you stay motivated during life's challenges and struggles.

You can choose to love everything about yourself. No matter how negative you may perceive certain aspects of yourself to be, you can decide you are completely worthy of love and treat yourself accordingly. This is radical acceptance.

ELEMENT 3:

SELF-WORTH

Your self-worth is your decision about your right to exist and feel valuable, no more and definitely not less than anyone else.

There is nothing you need to do to attain self-worth but decide you have it. It is not something that can be measured. It simply is.

When you make the decision, you will know it. It will be distinct from all that you have achieved in your life so far. While your achievements may or may not have assisted you in getting to that point, in the moment of truly owning your worth, you will know that it is not because of any of those things. You will know that you are someone of worth simply because you are someone. There's no logic to it. You simply go from being unworthy to being worthy because you decide it is so and it was always so, even if you couldn't see it before.

In Alice Walker's novel *The Color Purple*, Celie has an experience of claiming her right to exist and to be worthy of love and respect. Like Celie, when we have an experience of claiming our worth, it can feel very foreign if we've spent a lifetime undervaluing ourselves. Even as Celie is expressing her value, she is not really sure where her words are coming from. She experiences that the words seem to come from the trees, that air rushes into her mouth and shapes the words. Finally she declares to her oppressive husband, "I'm poor, I'm black, I may be ugly and can't cook, but I'm here.[8]"

After a lifetime of oppression, abuse and disrespect, Celie decides she is worth more, if for no other reason than she exists.

Some will disagree with me and say, 'No, I got my self-worth because I fought for it. I failed and failed but each time I got back up and tried again and my self-worth came out of those strivings.' That fighting and striving is certainly part of your journey and part of every human's journey, but what you are actually fighting for is the right to make the decision. You feel you need to prove that you have the right. But you don't need to fight for something that you already own and that can never be taken from you. If you still feel like you are fighting some days or every day to claim your self-worth, then you haven't yet made the decision. Once you make that decision, there is no more need to prove and there is no more fighting or debating within yourself anymore.

"I know my worth. I embrace my power. I say if I'm beautiful. I say if I'm strong. You will not determine my story; I will."

– Amy Schumer

Why do so many people have low self-worth?

Everybody deals with self-worth issues to some degree. For some of us, it's a major impediment.

Why is that?

It's possibly a flaw in our human nature: we are so in need of love and when we don't receive it from others in the way we want, we question whether we are worthy of it rather than giving it to ourselves.

But why is our default to question our self-worth? Why isn't it part of our nature to ignore negativity and retain good self-worth? Who really knows?! Maybe in another forty thousand years, we humans will have developed a nature like that.

What we do know is that doubts about our self and our worth usually develop when we're young. As we discussed in the **self-knowledge** chapter, those doubts are added to the map we carry into adulthood, causing us to constantly question ourselves. We continue to live by that map unless we decide to change it.

Parents unconsciously teach self-doubt to their children. Of course, children don't learn so much from what they are told as they do from what is modelled for them. Even if you had the best parents or you did the best job as a parent, at some point children absorb messages from the outer world – and aren't they often a bit (or a lot) screwed up?!

A distorted definition of self-love is common, with the term often confused with conceit, narcissism, vanity or selfishness. Even the dictionary lists these terms as synonyms of 'self-love'. I don't remember the first time I perceived it was a bad thing to value or love myself. I do recall messages in various forms about my body being shameful and bodily functions being something to be embarrassed about.

Additionally, we go our whole lives with virtually no escape from the media, including digitally altered images, body-shaming and a never-ending list of requirements you need to meet if you are to be considered worthy of love. In the words of Naomi Wolf, author of *The Beauty Myth*, "We as women are trained to see ourselves as cheap imitations of fashion photographs, rather than seeing fashion photographs as cheap imitations of women."

Fortunately, we are seeing more people take a stand against the media's portrayal of women and mainstream messages about worthiness. These more positive messages are usually welcomed, as indicated by the thousands of messages of support that actress Jennifer Aniston received for her July 2016 article in the Huffington Post. Fed up with constant media scrutiny, Aniston wrote:

> *"If I am some kind of symbol to some people out there, then clearly I am an example of the lens through which we, as a society, view our mothers, daughters, sisters, wives, female friends and colleagues. The objectification and scrutiny we put women through is absurd and disturbing. The way I am portrayed by the media is simply a reflection of how we see and portray women in general, measured against some warped standard of beauty. Sometimes cultural standards just need a different perspective so we can see them for what they really are — a collective acceptance ... a subconscious agreement. We are in charge of our agreement. Little girls everywhere are absorbing our agreement, passive or otherwise. And it begins early.*

The message that girls are not pretty unless they're incredibly thin, that they're not worthy of our attention unless they look like a supermodel or an actress on the cover of a magazine is something we're all willingly buying into. This conditioning is something girls then carry into womanhood."

These words express insight into the pervasive messages, both conscious and unconscious, that we are subjected to from a young age.

The media is a powerful force. And so many people, knowingly or not, are buying into the propaganda and sensationalised stories. We are constantly fed the messages of too fat, too thin, too pretty, too ugly, too old, too young, too [whatever]. It's a never-ending stream of messages about what you must do and who you must be in order to be accepted and the bar has been set very high. It can be challenging to rise above the pressure. Is it possible we just can't win?!

The good news is that self-worth isn't about winning – it's about deciding. Regardless of all the messages you have been force fed, at some point, if you want to be free, you will need to make a decision about your worth as a human being.

"A culture fixated on female thinness is not an obsession about female beauty, but an obsession about female obedience."

– Naomi Wolf

What does high self-worth actually look like?

High self-worth is not the same as vanity, conceit or narcissism. So what does it actually look like when you have a sense of self-worth?

Some of the signs include:

- **You take care of yourself.** When you believe you're valuable, you look after yourself. You maintain the standards you hold for yourself and the boundaries you hold others to because it is ultimately more important for you to have good mental, emotional, physical and spiritual health than it is for you to keep others happy. You understand that you can't give to others what you don't already have, so you take care of yourself in ways that bring you joy and empower you to serve others if you choose. By contrast, when you lack self-worth, you over-commit, over-give, over-compensate and over-excuse. You also stay much longer than you know you should in desperate, hurtful or harmful situations.

"The greatest gift you can give to somebody is your own personal development. I used to say, "If you will take care of me, I will take care of you." Now I say, "I will take care of me for you, if you will take care of you for me.""

– Jim Rohn

- **You have quality relationships**. When you value yourself, you will not tolerate poor treatment from others. You communicate your boundaries and desires. This causes some people to improve the way they interact with you and others to remove themselves from your life. Either way, the quality of your relationships improves. You understand there are some relationships that you don't enjoy but that can't be removed from your life. Your healthy self-worth means you can be in the company of these people if necessary, but not be emotionally triggered by their words and behaviours. You'd rather put your energy into relationships that bring joy.

"The person with adequate self-esteem doesn't feel hostile toward others. They aren't out to prove anything, they can see facts more clearly, and aren't as demanding in their claims on other people."

– Maxwell Maltz

- **You are incomparable.** High self-worth means you spend little time comparing yourself to others. Caroline McHugh described this way of being as having an interiority complex. [9] Unlike a superiority complex (when you think you are the most important person around) or an inferiority complex (where you have overmodest self-worth and tend to self-deprecate), with an interiority complex you don't need to focus on other people in order to make comparisons. It's more important you are always growing and becoming better than you were before, rather than needing to feel like you're better than others.

"When you find yourself judging another person, think in terms of 'is this a self-esteem issue?' Because it is."

– Caroline Myss

- **Approval is unnecessary.** People with high self-worth enjoy approval and love to receive compliments and praise. They are also usually better at receiving and giving compliments – unlike those with low self-worth who often don't believe compliments when they receive them. The important distinction is that while people with self-worth enjoy praise, they don't fall apart when they don't get it. In the absence of approval, they can approve of themselves. Of course, people with high self-worth will face challenges and setbacks, like everyone else, but those experiences do not diminish their sense of worth.

- **You can speak your truth and stay open to feedback from others.** High self-worth means you can stay in communication with others, even when it's challenging, because you know your worth is not determined by their words. You can say what you need to say without being aggressive and you can hear what others have to say without needing to be defensive – common reactions from those who source their worth from external sources. It is interesting to note these two kinds of reactions are usually correlated; the day that you can speak your truth is the same day that you will be able to stay present to the truth of others. While rarely easy, the **courage** to stay with truth is evidence that someone has done work on themselves and their sense of self-worth.

"Show me a woman who can actually sit with a man in real vulnerability and fear, I'll show you a woman who's done incredible work. You show me a man who can sit with a woman who's just had it; she can't do it all anymore ... and he really listens. I'll show you a guy who's done a lot of work."

– Brene Brown

- **Perfect is unnecessary.** With high self-worth, the need for life to be perfect falls away. Perfectionism is usually motivated by worrying about what other people will think. The internal motivation of people with high self-worth creates healthy striving, driven by the need to be better for themselves.

- **You can let things go.** People with high self-worth are better at letting things go. People with low self-worth attach their worth to external rewards or people. Unfortunately, when those things leave, they feel their worth is diminished. This creates susceptibility to neediness or desperation. People with high self-worth don't need to hold on to anything for validation. They know that everything they really need is available, so there is no need to force things or people to stay.

- **You feel full.** High self-worth is more than just feeling complete – you feel abundant. You feel a sense of fullness, completely the opposite of the scarcity associated with low self-worth. When you really believe you are lovable and valuable, it creates an **energy** that you want to do something with, either with other people or on your own.

"Your worth is beyond perception because it is beyond doubt."

– A Course in Miracles

Creating self-worth

While creating self-worth might be as simple as making a decision, it is rarely easy. Some unlearning is needed as well as experimenting with new ways of being. Continual reinforcement is also required until thoughts and feelings of self-worth become a natural part of life. Here are some suggestions to help you enhance your self-worth.

Begin from wherever you are

Self-worth is about loving and accepting yourself, regardless of everything you are or are not.

The moment you give yourself a hard time for doing anything that indicates low self-worth, you're missing the point of self-worth.

Wherever you are is where you are. In every situation you faced in your life, you did the best you knew how to at the time. Maybe you look back and think, 'I know I could have done better.' Maybe – except you didn't. Now that you have new information, you can choose to do life differently.

Self-worth can start today, no matter your current situation.

Remember, a sign of high self-worth is being able to let things go.

Your past does not dictate your future or assign any value to your worth as a person. Remind yourself of this any time you say or do something that indicates low worth. You can simply acknowledge what you have done, make corrections as necessary and move on.

If you were rude to another person, for example, you could acknowledge it. You could apologise. You could ask the other person what they need in order to repair any damage to the relationship. But throughout all of this, you can choose to know that your words and your actions do not determine your worth any more than someone else's words and actions determine theirs. Keep reminding yourself of this.

Whatever happened before this moment, even if it was something you did five minutes ago, does not define who you are in this moment. Each new moment is another opportunity to claim your self-worth; to decide you are worthy.

"No matter what age you are, or what your circumstances might be, you are special, and you still have something unique to offer."

– Barbara de Angelis

Accept ALL of you

Self-worth means valuing all of you – not just the parts you like or that you think are worthy of approval.

These parts are easy to appreciate, aren't they? We happily show those parts of ourselves to the world.

But what about those parts of us that we judge as wrong, or that we assume will be judged negatively by others? We all have parts of ourselves that we deem inappropriate, sinister, gross, weak or deviant. We usually hide those parts from others and we often hide them from ourselves as well.

Psychologist Carl Jung referred to the denied parts of ourselves as 'the shadow', a term that is now regularly used in psychology. Each person's shadow is individual to themselves and can include socially or religiously deprecated emotions such as selfishness, lust, greed, envy or anger.

There is a problem with attempting to deny your shadow though... it won't be denied!

As Jung explained, the shadow regularly makes its presence known indirectly. Any time you judge another person, it is likely you are projecting your own shadow onto them. Any time you act impulsively, the impulse may be coming from your shadow. Whenever you numb your emotions, you're most likely attempting to silence the voice of your shadow.

Enacting these kinds of behaviours doesn't sound like personal freedom, does it?

That's because it's not.

This doesn't stop us from trying though. As a society, we have learned numerous ways to avoid, numb or distract ourselves from the shameful or painful parts of ourselves, including painkillers, alcohol, shopping, food, sex or [insert your preferred numbing tactic here]. According to Brene Brown's research, we have become the most in-debt, obese and medicated adults in human history.[10] In many cases, we numb to the point of addiction.

Numbing is not for you if you want to grow and experience personal freedom. At best, the numbing offers you some reprieve. Sometimes, this is just what you need. Like when my apartment flooded while I was writing this book. It was a disaster and I felt overwhelmed just thinking about what needed to be done to resolve the mess. Surrounded by an apartment in shambles, no chair to sit on and a looming book deadline, I stood at the kitchen sink and ate chocolate ice cream straight out of the container. It was the perfect comfort food to provide me with a few moments of escape from the challenge at hand. A well-managed reprieve like this when you're dealing with a challenge is sometimes healthy and can help with pain or stress, but it is never a long-term strategy.

> "In an emotion-phobic culture, most of us don't know how to listen very well to emotional pain for the simple reason that we have never been taught that doing so is a good thing, or how to do it. In school, about all we learn about 'negative' emotions is that displaying them is bad conduct. We're taught little about what these emotions are or how they work. In religious institutions, we're often taught that fear, despair, or anger is a sign of sin or insufficient faith."

– Miriam Greenspan

A devil named Ita Rita

Joseph Campbell once said, "A devil is a God who has not been recognised." After all I've now learned about 'the shadow', I understand what he meant. When I first heard it though, while curious, I couldn't really appreciate it – not until I chose to meet a part of my own shadow.

I had learned a bit about the shadow conceptually and I was curious to understand more. So I decided to give a name to the parts of myself I disliked or felt ashamed of. I wanted to understand this part of me that seemed so negative, hurtful, or unforgiving. She seemed ugly to me. Logically, I thought she needed an ugly name. Almost in the same moment as I was asking the question, 'What is the ugliest name I could give her?' the name Ita Rita came to mind.

Ita Rita was the name of the doll I was given for my eighth birthday. I loved this doll and was so excited when I discovered that my parents had given me exactly what I had asked for. My excitement was dampened when I looked at the birth certificate my doll came with and learned that my doll's name was Ita Rita. Why would they give my beautiful doll such an ugly name? (My apologies to anyone named Ita or Rita – clearly I wasn't driven by the desire to be unique at that time in my life.)

I posted my request to the toy manufacturer to issue a new birth certificate. It arrived a short time later and the name Ita Rita was never to be mentioned again until two and a half decades later when I wondered what to name this ugly part of myself. In that moment she was known as Ita Rita, the ugliest name I could imagine. Then some interesting things began to happen. Perhaps because she now had a name, I began to think of her as a person. I began talking to her, rather than repressing her. I wasn't particularly nice to her. But treating her like a person was an improvement on treating her like... I'm not even sure how to describe how I used to treat her. Like something to be ashamed of, perhaps like mould in the bathroom that needs to be removed before guests visit.

So Ita Rita went from being something like bathroom mould to being a despicable person. I would occasionally lower myself with snobby arrogance to her level so that we could converse. Then some even more interesting things began to happen. Ita began to seem strangely human. The more I spoke with her, the more I learned about her. She often seemed like a scared little girl. She was mostly driven by the need to feel safe. She was quite secretive and slow to trust people, and that seemed to be because she was the keeper of shameful secrets.

I continued conversing with Ita Rita. It wasn't like a scene from a movie, where the actor is conversing with an invisible person and strangers observing think they are crazy. Of course I knew I was simply speaking with another part of myself, but it was a part of me that I had tried to deny because it made me feel ashamed. In hindsight, there was no sense to it. I was treating a part of myself as less-than-human. So the act of speaking to this part of me like she had the same worth as any human being, even if I didn't like her, had a profound impact on me. It changed how I viewed my worth because I could now see that all parts of me deserved a sense of worth, not just the parts I had previously termed 'acceptable'.

Ita Rita embodied everything about me that I thought was unlovable and now I loved her. I valued her strength and appreciated her purpose in keeping me safe. She also helped me to see how strongly I was impacted by judgements placed on me and societal expectations about how to behave – for if it weren't for all those judgements, there would have been no need to deny her in the first place.

"The most terrifying thing is to accept oneself completely."

– Carl Jung

Radical Acceptance

The greatest gift you will ever give yourself is a fully accepted, whole and integrated you.

You can choose to love everything about yourself. No matter how negative you may perceive certain aspects of yourself to be, you can decide you are completely worthy of love and treat yourself accordingly.

This is radical acceptance.

This is an uncommon journey given the way people tend to avoid looking at the parts of themselves they don't like. But it is also one of the most powerful steps you will take towards your freedom.

There are no specific rules about how to take the journey to radical acceptance. If you can simply make the choice and then live accordingly, then do it. Don't wait another day. If you struggle with making this choice, then take it one step at a time, and never stop. Any step that reinforces your self-worth will do. It doesn't necessarily mean sitting with a therapist. That works for many people and I'm an advocate myself, but don't let a distaste for therapy be a barrier to getting to know deeper parts of yourself. Other options might be to talk with a trusted friend or attend a workshop that develops your self-acceptance. Or perhaps you would like to name those parts of yourself that you tend to deny, like I did. It still seems to me like a silly exercise sometimes, but I don't care because it worked and it helped to set me free.

Treat yourself like a cherished friend

If you're unsure where to begin with creating more self-worth, you could start by treating yourself as a cherished friend. Women especially have a tendency to put others before themselves. We have been brainwashed into believing that our worth depends on how much we cater to the needs of others. When we do choose to give to ourselves, we often have to negotiate with the guilt that goes along with that choice.

Decide that you are as valuable as a cherished friend. Whatever you would give to them, you should also give to yourself. You can begin with kind words rather than the criticism to which you regularly subject yourself. Would you speak to a cherished friend that way? Of course not, so don't do it to yourself either. And would you expect so much of a cherished friend that they end up feeling exhausted and drained? No, you wouldn't. So why do you put so many expectations on yourself that you end up feeling that way?

Decide to treat yourself with worth. When unsure, simply ask: How would I treat a cherished friend right now?

Brainwash yourself (in a good way!)

We're all brainwashed.

When most people hear the term 'brainwashing', they think of something negative. However, another way of thinking about it is that we are all brainwashed and it is not necessarily positive or negative.

Advertisers are constantly attempting to manipulate us to think and behave in the way they want. We are constantly exposed to messages about how we should look. Over and over, we see digitally altered images of women leading us to constantly question how we compare to those unrealistic images.

Some of the messages might be good if they help us – like warnings about the negative effects of smoking. There's also the more innocent kind of brainwashing we all receive from our parents and other caregivers who are simply trying to ensure we behave in ways they deem appropriate.

Positive or negative, there are some ideas that are fed to us over and over again. We receive these messages constantly – and they're brainwashing us.

We could logically deduce that if some form of brainwashing has contributed to your low self-worth, then high self-worth could be created that way too. I found this to be true after buying an audiobook on self-esteem by Caroline Myss.[11] Over a five year period, I must have listened to it about 100 times. Eventually her words began to sink into my brain. I recognised that I was not behaving like someone with self-esteem. So I started trying some of her suggestions.

At first the new ways of being seemed foreign to me – I felt like a fraud; like I was just pretending. I kind of was. But was it any different to all the brainwashing I got from my parents and other grownups about being polite? The first times I said "please" and "thank you", I wasn't being polite; I was just doing as I was told. Now being polite feels very natural and appropriate to me. Similarly, after all my deliberate self-brainwashing, it now seems normal for me to treat myself to a guilt-free massage or respond to compliments with a simple "thank you". I've also learned to raise my standards about who I spend my time with and I've noticed warning bells go off in my mind if I do something to let myself down in the area of self-worth. It's just not who I am anymore.

You can do this too. You might as well, for if you're going to be brainwashed anyway, why not be brainwashed the way you want?!

How can you brainwash yourself? Here are some ideas to get started:

- **Audiobooks.** This is one of my favourites. In addition to being great for learning and entertainment, personal development and spirituality audiobooks are great for brainwashing. You can listen to them while you are driving, exercising, sleeping in, washing the dishes, sitting on a train, waiting for a friend who is late for lunch or doing housework.

- **Positive media.** Mainstream media contains mostly negative, fear-promoting information. It could be that people consume it because that is all the mainstream media makes readily available to us, or perhaps the media creates that content because that's what sells. Either way, you can do without it, or at least consume it in moderation to reduce the risk of negative brainwashing. There is plenty of positive media available; you just need to be more proactive about sourcing it. For example, you can buy magazines about healthy living, entrepreneurship, success, spirituality, gardening and sports, to name a few. These aren't too hard to find and you could try subscribing. Instead of automatically turning on the entertainment channel when you get home, opt for something more inspiring, perhaps via the Internet if it's not available on your TV. I often choose to watch TED talks via the internet and I find that a much more empowering and inspiring option than mainstream media.

- **People.** Be wise about who you spend your time with. The more time you spend with people, the more likely you are to be like them. If you spend time with people with high self-worth it will naturally rub off on you.

- **Reminders.** Do you need to set an alarm on your phone to remind you to do things that support your self-worth? Or put notes on your fridge? Reminders work really well for some people.

Finally, remember that you are aiming to brainwash yourself – as the word implies, you will be absorbing the same material more than once. Don't necessarily expect to read one book or watch one positive presentation and have your self-worth restored. With especially stubborn negative habits, you might need a lot of repetition because it can take a while before the message that you have worth finally sinks in (remember you've had years of negative brain washing!) If you're anything like I was, then low self-worth is a habit that needs breaking and it will take more than one listen over an extended period of time – as well as implementing what you learn every day – to create a permanent change. To this day, that brainwashing is one of the best things I've ever done.

Let people opt out of your life

Even when you show up to life as your most awesome and authentic self, some people will not be impressed or interested. I experienced this after getting back together with an ex-boyfriend for a short period of time. Friends were sceptical about the notion of getting back together with an ex. In my mind, as long as he was being good to me, as long as I was valuing myself as well as him, and as long as we were behaving as a partnership, I had no reason not to give the relationship another try.

Our first time together, I gave up too much of myself. I tend to be a very conscientious person, very aware of the needs of others, and I'm proactive about accommodating those needs. This is a great strength, but I'm also at risk of being drained if my partner isn't meeting me somewhere around the halfway point. Not long after we moved in together, I started to feel that I was being taken for granted. I attempted to communicate my needs unsuccessfully. Even though it was difficult to leave someone I loved very much, and who I believed loved me, I also knew I needed to leave if I wanted to live by my values and experience the kind of life that was important to me.

About nine months after our breakup, my ex began pursuing me again and he put in a lot of effort. He took me out for an amazing birthday dinner (something I did not experience while we were living together) and booked an overseas trip for the two of us. He was treating me really well and we were having a lot of fun together. My hopes were up. I loved him a lot.

What I really wanted to do differently this time was love and value myself as well as him. I wanted partnership. I wanted interdependence. I wanted two people who, when together, were greater than the sum of their parts. I wanted him to be free to chase his dreams and I wanted to be his champion, cheering and supporting him as he did. And I wanted someone who would simultaneously be that champion for me.

Part of the problem the first time we were in a relationship was that I stopped showing love to myself. I stopped being my own champion. When I reflect back, I know I can take **responsibility** for not nurturing my own needs as much as I nurtured his. We do teach people how to treat us and if I'm not treating myself well, then what am I teaching my partner about how to treat me?

This time I said it would be different. And it was. There were times I said no to requests for my time or energy – requests I would have agreed to in the past. This challenged me. I'm naturally a giving person and I wanted his approval, but I was determined to learn from my past and not make the same mistakes. Occasionally, I gave a bit more than I wanted but otherwise the relationship was good and I felt it was working. I was valuing and loving myself more and it really seemed like a win for both of us. I experienced how loving myself more meant having more love for him too. From a place of self-worth, I seemed to have more love in general and he was the person I most wanted to share it with.

While it would have been so easy to get carried away with these feelings, I also sought to maintain my rational self (perhaps, ironically, being more rational was something my boyfriend had taught me). I was aware that, while he was treating me really well and it was exciting, he had also treated me with a lot of appreciation at the beginning of our first time together. So I was in no rush. I felt we could go slower and build something stronger, something that looked a lot more like an interdependent partnership than either of us had ever experienced before.

That was until he called about a week before our overseas trip to say, "I'm not into the relationship." I was speechless but not totally surprised. He had seemed a little distant for a few days, though he hadn't expressed any concern until now. Part of me wanted to cry. I got a sick feeling in my stomach and I could feel my heart breaking. He didn't want to give me much explanation and it was tempting to try and force him to. Instead, as I stood there holding the phone, I reminded myself, 'I said I would give this relationship another chance as long as he was being good to me and we were behaving as partners.' In that moment, he was no longer doing either of those things.

I felt torn. I knew that a life of self-worth and living my values was what I wanted. But I would have preferred that life with him in it. I didn't have a choice over whether I could keep him and I refused to value myself any less. In spite of knowing I was heading towards the pain that inevitably goes with a broken heart, I knew it was the only way forward if I was valuing myself.

I noticed something very interesting over the following days as my heartache began to subside. The first time we ended our relationship, I had a lot of pain. Some of it was because I missed the person I loved but most of the pain was because I mourned the self that I had let go of in order to be in the relationship. This second time that we ended our relationship, I still felt pain due to the loss of someone I loved, but I had none of the pain associated with losing myself.

I felt empowered. I had learned a lot about the type of person I wanted to be within a relationship and I had new insights about the type of person I would need to be with if I wanted to create a partnership. By the end of those few days post-breakup, I was feeling really positive about how I had shown up to the relationship, as someone of value and worthy of partnership and love. I had shown up as my best self and yet... he opted out.

We had a long chat about a week later. Much of what he said confirmed he was not interested in mutual championing and interdependence at that point in his life. I guessed he preferred me as someone who was willing to give up her own needs. It was a challenging thing to accept. I still miss him some days. But I no longer have to deal with missing myself. I also see what a gift it was to experience showing up as my best self with the same person, rather than with someone new. It reaffirmed that who I am in a relationship is my choice, not dependent on the other person. I also learned that I can't change someone, but I can let them opt out.

If you're not willing to let people opt out of your life, you will end up compromising yourself in an effort to make them stay. When you do that, it's like saying, 'My authentic self is not worthy of having you in my life so I am going to attempt to compensate by being something I am not.' There is no freedom in that way of thinking.

It's not true that you're not worthy if someone chooses not to stay in your life. As happened to me, when you show up to life as your most authentic and best self, no matter how amazing you are, some people will opt out. Not everybody wants to hang out with you. Ouch! Stings a bit, doesn't it?

While I have the urge right now to say to you, 'You're awesome, and who needs them anyway,' I think it's important to just sit with the sting of this truth for a bit: Not everybody wants to hang out with you. You need to understand this if you want personal freedom, because it's the avoidance of this discomfort that will have you hanging around in places (real or metaphorical) longer than you should.

There could be many reasons why some people are not interested in co-creating a relationship with you. However, the reason is not really important because it's not ultimately about you. The other person just happens to be at a different place on their journey. All you really need to know is that it's not because there is anything 'wrong' with you.

You become less effective in life when your focus is on avoiding the sting of someone not valuing you. It's a bit like avoiding the discomfort of getting out of your warm bed on a cold morning. Sure, you could stay in bed every time you don't feel like getting up, but there will likely be some consequences, some of which you will probably regret. You need to get up and live the life that is waiting for you.

Of course, the pain of losing a relationship you want to keep is more painful than the discomfort of getting out of a warm bed on a cold morning. That's because you are biologically hardwired to need people, and relationships are important to your health, if not your survival. Hence, it can trigger a fear response when someone leaves. This is natural, but you need to learn to be with the discomfort.

I'm not saying you don't need people in your life. You really do. You just don't need *all* people in your life. And you definitely don't need someone who has made it clear, directly or indirectly, that they don't want you in their life. You really don't need them or that dynamic. You will survive without them. You might want them, but want them from afar and move on with your life, being your authentic self and creating the life you imagine. If you learn to do that well, you'll find that your desire for that other person dissipates as your life is filled with new opportunities – and people who choose to opt in! If that other person is meant to be in your life, they will return. And having someone who wants to be with the authentic you is a million times more enjoyable than someone who doesn't appreciate you the way you are.

This kind of wisdom can also be found in the works of Ralph Waldo Emerson. His words are more than a century old, but truth stands the test of time:

> "It has seemed to me lately more possible than I knew to carry a friendship greatly, on one side, without due correspondence on the other. Why should I cumber myself with regrets that the receiver is not capacious? It never troubles the sun that some of his rays fall wide and vain into ungrateful space, and only a small part on the reflecting planet. Let your greatness educate the crude and cold companion. If he is unequal, he will presently pass away; but thou art enlarged by thy own shining."

Emerson, by my translation, speaks of being your best self, leading by example, and being vulnerable in the face of the unknown. When you're true to your values, those friends to whom you are most suited will make a home in your heart. Those on a different path will walk on while you keep the lessons from your experiences and the knowledge that you allowed your best self to shine.

"I think it's very healthy to spend time alone. You need to know how to be alone and not be defined by another person."

– Oscar Wilde

"I've realised that for me to grow, I've got to let go."

– Rebecca Ferguson

Get therapy or coaching

I'm an advocate for therapy and coaching as a way of becoming empowered and improving my mental health. It makes good sense to me and I regularly see the benefits in myself and others. In the same way that a desire to improve my physical health might lead me to a physiotherapist or personal trainer, a commitment to my mental health leads me to someone with the skills to assist with that, usually a psychologist or a coach depending on my specific needs.

Around sixteen years ago when I was dealing with panic attacks, my psychologist was invaluable. I am so grateful for the safe space that she created for me to share the memories and thoughts I had long tried to avoid dealing with. As I discussed earlier in this chapter, repressed thoughts rarely just go away. They eventually show up somehow. In my case, they showed up as panic attacks and behaviours that reflected my low self-worth. My psychologist helped me to explore why I had undervalued myself and clarify what I really wanted for my life.

Over the years, I have also worked with several different coaches. They all assisted me to clarify my goals, held me accountable when it came to creating them and challenged me when my own thought processes were getting in my way. I appreciate having a sounding board and someone to hold me accountable when I'm not living up to my word or my potential. As a coach myself, I have also witnessed on numerous occasions how the time spent addressing and refining mental processes has not only enabled clients to become unstuck, but allowed them to thrive as they began showing up as their best selves.

Professionals such as psychologists and coaches can be invaluable in assisting with self-worth issues. When properly skilled, they assist you to take ownership of all the ways you are being ineffective and empower you with new skills and insights to better deal with challenges and life in general.

A word of advice: Not every coach or therapist will be the right fit for you. Before you engage their services, ensure you have found someone who can create a space safe enough for you to be vulnerable and open, while at the same time being willing to be honest with you. You should give yourself permission to do research and ask questions to determine whether you have found the right person, because they will be assisting you with the most important work you will ever take on – the development of you.

Chapter summary

- Your self-worth is your decision about your right to exist and feel valuable, no more and definitely no less than anyone else. There is nothing you need to do for your self-worth but decide you have it.

- There is no personal freedom without self-worth.

- We go our whole lives with virtually no escape from the media's never-ending list of requirements that we need to meet to be considered worthy of love. But regardless of all the messages are force fed, at some point, if we want to be free, we need to make a decision about our self-worth.

- When someone has high self-worth, they take care of themselves, they have quality relationships, they don't compare themselves to others, they don't need external approval, they speak their truth, they don't feel the need to strive for perfection, they can let things go, they are not judgmental and they feel full from within.

- When someone doesn't have self-worth, they will over-commit, over-give, over-compensate and over-excuse. They will also stay much longer than they should in desperate, hurtful or harmful situations.

- All of us have parts we embrace and parts we deny. A key element of self-worth is being able to accept all of those parts of you, even the ones you try to hide.

- Positive brainwashing can have a big impact on your level of self-worth, and negative brainwashing is often the culprit for low self-worth.

- People with high self-worth allow people to opt out of their life. They understand that if they show up in life as their most authentic self, some people will opt out and this says nothing about their value.

- Self-worth is an ongoing journey; it's important to embrace where you are now rather than making yourself wrong for anything that has happened in the past.

Energy is your most valuable resource. It's more valuable than time because your energy levels determine how you spend your time.

ELEMENT 4:

ENERGY

Resistance is a bitch.

It's a bitch that showed up regularly while writing this book, even though I loved writing it. I loved it so much that you'd think it should have been effortless. At times it was, but there were also plenty of times when it was a challenge to keep going in order to meet a deadline or to simply get it finished. It's like this with anything worth pursuing – no matter how passionate you are about it, you will eventually meet resistance because motivation, and even inspiration, can only take you so far.

I often feel called to do things I know will grow or challenge me. When I feel that desire within me, my freedom feels limited until I begin pursuing whatever I am called to. This is different to attempting to achieve something because of external opinions.

When I pursue things for external validation it tends to reduce my feelings of freedom. But when the pursuit of an internal calling begins, feelings of freedom increase. For example, I felt my freedom lay on the other side of finishing this book, or on the other side of finishing my degree, or on the other side of completing 2,000 hours of coaching. I felt that if I didn't get to the other side of these things, I would be captive to a lifetime of 'what ifs'. For clients I've worked with, freedom might lie on the other side of building their business, spending a year living overseas, raising a family, completing their first marathon or finally getting up the **courage** to say 'no' to a life that no longer works for them.

In the process of my clients and I getting to the other side of whatever we are called to do, we all eventually meet resistance.

Steven Pressfield describes resistance powerfully in his book *The War of Art*:[12]

> *"Resistance cannot be seen, touched, heard, or smelled. But it can be felt. We experience it as an energy field radiating from a work-in-potential. It's a repelling force. It's negative. Its aim is to shove us away, distract us, prevent us from doing our work."*

The only way we are going to be able to take on the force that is resistance is to generate greater levels of energy within ourselves. And we need to keep generating energy because our energy levels are constantly being depleted and resistance will continue to show up as long as we are pursuing our potential and our freedom.

How free do you feel when you're tired?

And how often do you feel tired?

If you're like most of society, which seems to glorify busyness, then you regularly feel tired. And if you have people relying on you, as most of us do, you probably feel exhausted, at least some of the time.

I used to think that time was my most valuable resource. Once it's spent, it's gone. There is nothing I can do to create more than twenty-four hours in a day.

I also felt that, with so much to do, all I needed to get it all done was more time.

Now there's a losing battle! Remember the quote from the meaning chapter: 'Whenever I fight with reality, I always lose!' There is absolutely no point fighting reality about the number of hours I have in a day. That impossible-to-win battle will just drain my energy even more.

Time is the great leveller. All people have the same amount of time each day. If you think about the people you admire and the great things they have achieved, it's not because of the amount of time they had.

Time is not my most valuable resource. Energy is.

My energy determines how I spend my time. High energy levels mean better decision-making abilities, greater levels of willpower and the fuel for developing and engaging with all of your freedom elements. This leads to better results in all areas of your life.

On the other hand, without sufficient energy, you will find yourself succumbing to habitual behaviours, fears and resistance. Without energy, there is no willpower.[13] Without willpower, there is rarely freedom.

But this is the good news – you can influence your energy levels.

The two types of energy

There are two types of energy: body energy and mind energy.

Body energy relates to the physical body. When you feel energetic in your body, there is a sense that you have strength and it's easy to get up and move around.

Mind energy relates to your thoughts. When your mind is energetic, you have thoughts that get you moving, including inspired, optimistic and creative thoughts. You want to take action – to do or become something.

These two types of energy are inextricably linked. If you feed one type of energy it will have a positive impact on the other. Similarly, if you drain one, it will drain the other. I regularly noticed while writing this book that I would feel tired after several hours of sitting at a computer typing and staring at a screen. One afternoon I felt so tired I laid down for a nap. After about ninety minutes of resting and occasionally drifting off to sleep, I continued writing. I'd had plenty of sleep the night before so it seemed strange that I needed to sleep in the middle of the day. When I felt fatigued the next day, instead of napping, I rode to a friend's house and we played basketball for an hour. I then returned home and continued writing and was no less productive than the day before. It was immediately obvious that my desire to sleep on the first day had little to do with body energy – my mind needed the rest.

As both types of energy are required to fuel your freedom, it's important to create sustainable, healthy habits that generate energy.

Creating energy

I had some concerns about the recommendations listed in this chapter for increasing energy levels. I feared insulting you, my reader, because many of these suggestions are common sense. Yet I regularly encounter people who aren't following this advice, even though common sense tells them they should. They are too caught up in the busyness of their day-to-day lives.

With this in mind, throughout this chapter I'll be covering key areas where you can more effectively manage your mind and body energy.

As these areas influence each other, implementing suggestions about either of them will ultimately have a positive impact on both your mind and body.

Warning: Notice if you hear a voice in your mind saying, *'Yes, yes, I know all this.'* Who doesn't know already that they need a good diet, exercise and sleep?

Knowing about these things is fruitless if you're not actually implementing them. If you're already doing all of these energising activities, feel free to move on to the next chapter, knowing your high energy levels will assist you with your other freedom elements. If you're not already doing the things you know you should, begin thinking about them in the context of your freedom. Your freedom literally depends on having the energy to create and maintain it.

Trust yourself

Creating energy involves trusting yourself. It means letting go of what everyone else says you should do and having the **courage** to trust your intuition. While I am going to discuss ways of improving your energy levels, they are just a guide. **Self-knowledge** is essential for managing your energy levels because there is no one size fits all. You need to find the formula that works well for you.

This is not always easy in the age of information, with almost everyone sharing their opinion like it's a fact. I have knowledgeable people who I trust tell me it's good to include meat in my diet. Other sources that I believe to be reliable and trustworthy tell me meat is not good for me and increases my risk of cancer – and this is before I even begin contemplating the impact of meat-eating on animals and the environment. Some information sources tell me that I need to wear sunscreen to protect myself from skin cancer, and then others say the chemicals in sunscreen cause cancer. You will have your own examples of health and energy advice contradictions. It can be frustrating – we want to do the 'right' thing but how can we when much of the advice is contradictory?

You need to trust yourself. Getting too caught up in frustration and confusion about the 'right' way to create energy is energy draining – how ironic!

I really enjoy yoga and I once tried Bikram yoga because I kept hearing people talking about its benefits and how much they loved it. In spite of all of the health benefits I was hearing, my body just did not feel good in that hot room and I didn't enjoy it. I trusted that and went back to the style of yoga I enjoyed and that my body loves. I also tried eating fewer carbohydrates for a while because a good friend was telling me how much better it was making her feel. Turns out it suits me for dinnertime but doesn't work for me in the middle of the day. I would feel hungry again too soon after lunch and was then at risk of snacking on much less healthy foods. So I trusted how I felt both in my body and intuitively, and built a healthy, energising eating routine around that.

If you feel you need to sleep an hour more or less than is recommended, trust that. If you notice you lose energy by being around certain people, trust that too. If you notice you always feel better after going for a walk or a run, trust that.

Adhering to the rules of others is not what personal freedom is about. You are the expert on you – trust yourself.

Be honest with yourself

While I believe you are the expert on your life, I also feel it necessary to step in as devil's advocate. It's the coach in me wanting to check and ask: Are you trusting your most true self (i.e. the voice that speaks to you when you're not feeling afraid or lazy) or are you trusting the voice that supplies you with lots of excuses?

As human beings, we are excellent at creating excuses for why we can't do things – and often these are things we know we should do. But we don't do them because we are afraid – afraid of looking silly, afraid of failing, afraid of what others will say, afraid of [enter one of your most common excuses here].

Creating excuses about why you won't enjoy something, or can't do something even though you might enjoy it, does nothing to help you grow or enhance your freedom. For example, if you don't want to go swimming because you fear how you will look in a bathing suit, be honest about that. There is no freedom in missing out on activity that you think would be good for you and that you think you would enjoy because you feel embarrassed. So be honest about the 'real' reason you are making excuses because then you can tackle it directly and create a more empowering inner dialogue that sounds something more like: 'I let go of any real or imagined negative opinions others have of me. I have **self-worth** enough that I can put my happiness ahead of paying attention to the judgements of others and I know my health, energy and vitality are my **responsibility**.'

The same goes if you would like to try running a half-marathon and you tell yourself you can't – but the real reason you don't try is you're afraid of looking like a failure if you're unable to finish. Or if you think that you could benefit from meditation but you tell yourself you don't have the time. Or if you feel that smoking or eating sweet foods is essential because it relaxes you. If you are really honest with yourself about your excuses, what do you know to be true about your **self-worth** and your level of **responsibility** around the issue? What **meanings** are you attaching to the issue? What would you do if you had **courage**?

You don't have to share your honest thoughts and feelings with the whole world, but you do need to be at least honest with yourself. Discussing your thoughts and feelings with a trusted friend is often helpful too.

Test ideas

You can theorise that you will or will not enjoy a particular diet or exercise or other health practice, but you won't know until you actually try. So get out there and test your theories. Don't worry about investing a lot of money in having all the right gear. First, just give it a go. Have the **courage** to make a mistake. If you enjoy it, then you can increase your investment. If you don't enjoy it, move on knowing you have expanded your comfort zone.

Watch out for the 'I know' when considering a health practice you haven't actually tried. When I hear clients say, 'I know I should go out for a run,' or 'I know I should eat better,' or 'I know I should get more sleep,' or 'I know I should stop focusing on the opinions of others,' my response is usually the same: "No, if you knew it, you'd be doing it. Until then, you just theorise it."

I spent plenty of time 'knowing' I should eat better. Only when I actually took **responsibility** for my health and acted from a place of enough **self-worth** did I truly *know* how beneficial it was to eat better because I experienced my energy levels and quality of life go up.

Mind energy

For mind energy, you will need to take charge of your thoughts. You will need to reduce the thought patterns that limit your energy and increase those that improve your energy levels. This will include managing the **meanings** you create and taking steps to create **calm**.

Wilt

Susan remembers the moment when her inner voice gently said *'Should you be doing this?'*

'No', she thought, but went ahead and had the affair anyway.

After the affair began, Susan got another internal warning about what she was doing. 'I need to be honest and admit what I've done', she thought.

Susan chose to deny this though, instead telling herself *'No, I deserve this'* because she believed the man she was having an affair with was the key to her happiness.

She soon discovered how wrong she was. Every day before she was eventually caught out, Susan was wracked with guilt, not the happiness she'd imagined. She always had strong values about marriage. She was a Sunday School teacher and both her parents were marriage counsellors and deeply religious. Even though it was self-inflicted, Susan felt she couldn't live with the guilt. At its worst, she was having suicidal thoughts. At best, it preyed constantly on her mind, leaving her feeling drained and unable to live powerfully.

One of the most energy-draining and freedom-reducing thought patterns is wilt. Wilt is a combination of 'worry' and 'guilt'. I've blended the two words because I view guilt and worry as the same thought pattern except for one key difference – worry relates to the future and guilt relates to the past.

Wilt is the emotion that follows an initial warning. For example, that first thought Susan had, questioning her intended course of action, was her initial warning. All subsequent thinking about the issue and associated emotions was her guilt.

In the case of guilt, the initial warning is to let you know that something in the past should or could have been different. In the case of worry, the initial warning is a potentially negative outcome in the future.

The initial warning is very useful. It's the message you are sending yourself that something may need to change; either you need to do something differently or you need to change your perception. To continue following a wilt thought pattern beyond the initial warning, however, is rarely useful.

Regardless of what happened in the past or what could happen in the future, one thing is certain, worry or guilt won't change anything; it will only diminish your energy levels, use up your time and reduce your freedom. All the while, you are engaging in the false perception that you are doing something already and, therefore, don't need to take any real action.

Engage your **self-knowledge, courage** and **self-worth** and then ask yourself: How many points do I award myself because I give so much time and energy to worry and guilt?

Most people give themselves lots of points for worrying about other people or what will happen in the future, or for feeling guilty about something that happened in the past. You can give yourself as many points as you like, but in the end you still have to live with the energy-sapping awareness that your life is half-lived and the energy you've expended on worry and guilt didn't actually achieve anything.

The challenge is that it takes courage to rectify what happened in the past or act as your higher self in the future. It takes courage to be vulnerable and admit if you've done something wrong. And it often takes courage to move into the unknown that arises when you do something different, even risky, in order to create a more empowering future.

Rather than source the **courage**, people engage in wilt and pretend it's doing something useful. In reality, this pattern is useless and energy consuming. That the result of blending these two words is the word 'wilt' is just perfect. The word wilt means to lose strength. If you spend excessive amounts of time in guilt or worry, you will lose strength. Wilt thoughts will hold you captive in a freedom-reducing, time-wasting and energy-draining thought cycle.

How much extra energy, time and freedom would you have if you didn't spend them all on worry and guilt?

If you do want to take action on a warning about the past or the future but it's not possible or practical to do that right now, then park the issue and get on with something productive in your life. Don't waste your time and energy on an issue that you can't take action on right now.

Of course, taking action will take energy, whether it is changing something you are doing or just changing your perceptions. At first, this might seem like a lot more time, effort and energy than simply dedicating your thoughts to worry and guilt. To think like this, though, is too short term. The energy you spend on taking action and managing your perceptions is renewable energy. It will come back to you through the expansion of your spirit and the freedom you create. Energy spent on wilt will not return; it will just slowly drain you.

"Worry does not empty tomorrow of its troubles, it empties today of its strength."

– Corrie ten Boom

Meditation

Meditation is an excellent antidote to wilt thoughts as well as any other thoughts that drain you of vitality and freedom.

Meditation also enables us to slow down and be more conscious, both of which are conducive to more effective behaviours and outcomes. As Russell Simmons explains in *Success through Stillness*, "meditation gives our amygdala a chance to make more calm and measured assessments of situations.[14]" Without this discipline, the amygdala, which is housed in the brain and plays a key part in the fight or flight response, will be hypersensitive to threats. If your thought patterns are like this then you know how exhausting it can be.

I discuss meditation in greater detail in the chapter on **calm**.

Buddha was asked, "What have you gained from meditation?" He replied, "Nothing! However, let me tell you what I've lost: anger, anxiety, depression, insecurity and fear of old age and death."

Energising friends

You know there are some friends who energise you and some who drain you. It doesn't necessarily mean people who drain your energy are bad, any more than you are bad because there are some people for whom you are an energy drain. And the extent to which people drain energy can be contextual – there could be some people who energise you at work, but who might leave you feeling drained if you meet up socially. Sometimes we marry people who energise us at home, but who would drive us crazy if we had to work together. Our own children can be energising in some contexts and draining in others.

That said, there are some people who can be toxic for you. It's wise to keep your distance as long as the relationship is toxic. If you don't have a choice about that person being in your life, you can take **responsibility** for any ways you are co-creating the relationship.

As a general rule, choose friends who challenge your mind, encourage your spirit and protect your heart. These friends are true blessings and natural energy boosters.

Sense of meaning or purpose

If you don't have a sense of **meaning** or purpose, it's likely you'll feel challenged by the belief there is no end to life's struggles and this can make it hard to get motivated. Having meaning or purpose creates energy.

A sense of meaning makes you want to get out of bed in the morning because you're looking forward to another day engaged with whatever it is that fills you with meaning. You feel inspired – and inspiration has a way of creating energy out of nothing.

If you have an interest in your life that inspires you but you're not pursuing it, take time to explore why. You'll very likely find gaps in your other freedom elements. Strengthen those so you can pursue that which inspires you. It took a lot of **self-worth, courage** and **responsibility** for me to choose to pursue my calling as a career. While the experience challenged me and I was often afraid of failing, I also felt alive and excited to get out of bed each day.

I imagine it's that feeling of aliveness Amelia Earhart had when she was flying or even thought about flying. She got a great deal of meaning from being an advocate for female pilots and women's rights and from her flying goals, including numerous solo flights. Earhart came up against many challenges during her pursuits but she was so closely aligned with her dream that she simply had to keep pursuing it.

> *"What do dreams know of boundaries?"*
>
> **– Amelia Earhart**

When life is challenging, or seems to be at its worst, having a sense of meaning can provide us with the necessary energy to keep going, even though it may be hard. At these times, as discussed in the **meaning** chapter, we can forge meaning as a way to give our lives greater purpose and to gain the energy to keep going.

Being open to help

Managing negative or disempowering thoughts and their associated feelings is a challenge for all of us. At times, the challenge can escalate into a mental health issue, even if it's only once or twice in your lifetime. For some, however, it can be an ongoing struggle. Depression, for example, is estimated by the

World Health Organisation to affect 350 million people of all ages. Furthermore, over 800,000 people commit suicide every year, and this is the second leading cause of death in fifteen to twenty-nine year olds[15].

From my research, studies and experience, it seems a factor making this issue even worse is the social stigma associated with mental health issues. It can prevent people from reaching out to get the help they need – treatments that we know can help - because they don't want to be judged by those around them.

Dealing with these kinds of issues is crucially important for energy and personal freedom. In the words of writer and lecturer Andrew Solomon, "The opposite of depression is not happiness, but vitality.[16]"

Solomon, who suffered with debilitating depression and spoke openly about his battle, said that many sufferers know their depression is ridiculous even while they are experiencing it. So they would change it if they knew how. Unfortunately, many don't know how. Yet society treats them like they should know, making the condition worse. Solomon's research also unearthed a key difference between those who found a way past their depression and those who continued to suffer – the ability to own their experience. "Those who denied their experience," said Solomon, "were the ones most enslaved by it."

Therapy is one way to assist someone to own their experience. Treatments such as therapy can be highly effective, so if you are suffering from depression, or even prolonged sadness, then value yourself enough to ask for help. Nobody is saying this is easy; it absolutely takes **courage** to be vulnerable and say, "I'm struggling at the moment," or "I don't know what to do to improve how I'm feeling." However, your health and happiness are worthy aspirations and there are people who recognise this. So if the first person you seek help from is not obliging, then keep asking. You're worth it and your freedom depends on it.

Unfortunately, not everyone will be as helpful as you'd like. I once went to see a psychologist and it was a terrible experience because I felt misunderstood, judged and frustrated. Fortunately, I didn't let it put me off therapy altogether, and later found a more empathetic therapist. I encourage you to keep looking until you find a suitable professional or an objective friend, who can see your challenges from the outside. Because sometimes when you're in the middle of a problem, everywhere you look all you see is the problem. It's logical to acknowledge that someone on the outside is in a position to see things that you can't and provide you with an objective perspective.

If that feels like too much, you can start with this small step: Choose to free yourself from any stigma preventing you from getting the help you might need. No matter what you do in your life, people are going to criticise. Remember their criticisms are not about you. Their criticisms are a reflection of what exists within them. The numbers of those suffering from depression are so high that everyone will at some point either experience it personally or be close to someone who is going through it, so the stigma affects everyone in some way.

"Depression is the family secret that everyone has."

– Andrew Solomon

Body energy

Taking care of your body is important for having energy. We are going to cover some of the most important things you can do for creating energy in your body: exercise, eating a healthy diet, keeping hydrated and getting adequate sleep.

Exercise

Your body is designed to move. As Dr Christiane Northrup explains in her wonderful book *Goddesses Never Age*[17], you need to move so that your blood, lymph fluid and oxygen can all circulate. Of course, this won't be news. You've been living under a rock if you don't already know that exercise is good for you.

If you need more evidence though, research has found that exercise decreases perceived stress and emotional distress, and reduces smoking, alcohol and coffee intake. Not surprisingly, the research also found exercise to increase healthy eating and emotional control. Perhaps a little surprising was that participants in the study also undertook more household chores, attended to commitments, better monitored their spending and improved their study habits[18].

So move your body. It will energise you.

How much exercise should you do?

Do enough to make you feel good. Remember what I said about trusting yourself, being honest and testing ideas. And acknowledge that you will sometimes, or often, not want to exercise. This is a common feeling among humans and, if you trust it too often, you might never do any exercise! I still find it strange that I regularly feel resistance to exercise because I know that once I get moving I usually great. I actually find it quite annoying that I have to deal with resistance. But then I just accept resistance is part of the process and push through it. Mel Robbins explained that the energy required to push through resistance is called 'activation energy'[19]. It's the same initial push of energy that you need to force yourself to get up in the morning when your body would rather stay in a warm bed.

If you're also the sort of person who needs to engage activation energy to get moving in the face of resistance, practise doing this as often as you can. It doesn't mean you then have to run a marathon. You can just walk or do yoga in your living room or do some other exercise you enjoy. Sometimes I like to just turn up the music and dance around my house. The point is, the more you practise pushing through resistance when you know your body needs the exercise, the easier and more habitual it will become.

Do it because you value yourself (remember **self-worth** is your decision!) and because it will fuel your freedom.

Healthy diet

As my good friend and doctor of Chinese Medicine, Clare Pyers, says, "There are all kinds of vitamins and minerals that your body needs that can't be forgotten about without consequence. You are **responsible** for providing all the ingredients your body needs for good health, wellbeing and energy. If you're only providing half the ingredients, your body does its best to adapt but you're never going to achieve optimal health or energy."

The need to adhere to a healthy diet is as obvious as the need to do enough exercise. And like exercise, the right diet is also going to be unique to you. There are millions of different recipe books, health professionals and wellbeing websites that offer suggestions on the best diet. It can be overwhelming to do the 'right' thing, and preparing or purchasing healthy foods is not always convenient.

So while a healthy diet is important, it is equally important you avoid being stressed about it. There is no freedom in stressing.

Plus, if you stress, the stress hormones will likely just counteract all the positive action you take. So first relax, and then go back to:

- **Trust yourself:** After exploring options, what does your gut tell you it really needs in order provide you with good health and energy?

- **Be honest:** What are your real food habits and where do you need to improve?

- **Test:** How do different diets make your body feel?

Also keep in mind that this recommendation about managing your diet well is about creating energy, not about losing weight. As we discussed in the previous chapter, there are a lot of external expectations about how we are supposed to look. Managing your diet to adhere to a prescribed body shape is not what freedom is about. Freedom is loving your body and providing it with the fuel that shows how much you care about it.

One of my most important tips for healthy eating is to find ways to enjoy food that is good for you. If you feel overly constricted by your diet, then how much freedom do you have? When you feel free, you will find you naturally want to nourish your body because you truly value it. If you're not feeling a desire to nourish your body, I suggest reviewing your **self-worth** element. When you value yourself, you value your body and treat it accordingly, with foods that provide nourishment and pleasure.

One of the ways I made eating healthy food easier and more pleasurable was by purchasing a blender. At the time, it was quite an investment for me financially but I made the purchase based on my view of how important my health is and how worthy

I am. I use my blender regularly for healthy smoothies. One of my favourite smoothie recipes includes Brazil nuts, almonds and pumpkin seeds (all of which I never eat otherwise), broccoli (which I would never eat raw otherwise) and berries (yum!). Sometimes I add raw cacao for chocolate flavour. Instant healthy energy booster!

> *"People try to negotiate around not having to make diet changes. But you can't get a leave pass from your own body."*
>
> **– Dr Clare Pyers**

Water

Low energy is just one of the many symptoms associated with dehydration.

Feeling tired? Drink water.

Got a headache? Drink water.

Can't concentrate? Drink water.

Got the flu? Drink water.

Feeling moody? Drink water.

Dr Fereydoon Batmanghelidj M.D. is author of the book *Water: For Health, for Healing, for Life: You're Not Sick, You're Thirsty!* He suggests that asthma, allergies, arthritis, hypertension, depression, headaches, diabetes and obesity are just some of the conditions and diseases that are caused by persistent dehydration [20].

I don't know to what extent water can heal serious ailments, but common sense tells us that it's not going to hurt and it's very likely going to help. Think about all of the fluids in your body and how they serve the important purposes of clearing out toxins, healing your skin, digesting food or growing babies. Any and every function of the body will be assisted by adequate water.

I start every day with a 600ml bottle of water filled the night before. If you are one of those people who bounds out of bed each morning, I secretly envy you a little and you might not need to fill a water bottle the night before. Good preparation for me means that after waking, I simply reach for the bottle and drink. I do this leisurely and by the time I've finished I'm hydrated and feeling awake. Then I'm ready to bound energetically out of bed!

Drinking enough water is about creating the habit. When I first lived with my partner, he drank a lot of soda every day. He tried changing to water and struggled at first – his body wasn't used to the sugar reduction. Today he is a proud water drinker who has never felt or looked healthier, and that last box of soda cans remained unfinished for well over six months. He knows now that his past resistance to water was because of the habits he kept.

"I believe that water is the only drink for a wise man."

– Henry David Thoreau

Sleep

Adequate sleep is crucial for managing your energy levels and health in general. We seem to have some common sense about this and, according to neuroscientist Russell Foster, a profound amount of ignorance. As a society, we are sleep deprived.[21]

We think we will be better off if we can get more hours in the day by sleeping less. I remember getting on that bandwagon. Experience taught me that I might end up with a greater quantity of waking hours, but it will be at the cost of quality. I know I would not have written this book if I was sleeping less than my body required each night (as measured by waking up before my alarm each morning). My mind functions more effectively and my writing is more productive when I am well rested. When my sleep is insufficient, I might have more time but I also encounter a lot more resistance.

In his TED talk, Foster explains that sleep is not an indulgence. If you don't sleep, you don't function, sometimes with fatal results. A tired brain indulges in micro-sleeps and it's estimated that around thirty-one per cent of drivers will fall asleep at the wheel at least once in their lives, leading to thousands of accidents.

The list of issues due to lack of sleep goes on, including poor memory, less creativity, increased impulsiveness, poor judgement and increased risk of mental illness. A tired brain also craves stimulants to wake it up, leading many tired people to turn to drugs, caffeine and nicotine, all of which we know can have negative impacts on health, especially if used to excess.

Foster also reports that if you sleep around five hours or less every night, you have a fifty per cent likelihood of being obese. Sleep loss is connected to the rise of the hormone ghrelin, the hunger hormone, leading the brain to seek out carbohydrates, particularly sugars. Tired people are also more stressed and sustained stress leads to suppressed immunity. Increased stress levels combined with excess sugar is an excellent recipe for diabetes.

In another TED talk, neuroscientist Jeff Iliff explains the importance of sleep by likening it to leaving all the household chores until the weekend when you have time to do them. When your brain is awake, it is busy and puts off clearing away the waste. When you go to sleep, your brain shifts into a kind of cleaning mode. The brain's ongoing, intense, electrical activity uses up a quarter of the body's entire energy supply, even though the brain accounts for only about two per cent of the body's mass. All of this activity creates waste that the body needs to expel. It moves from the brain into the fluid surrounding the brain, then passes into the bloodstream to be filtered out of the body. This very important function only happens when you're sleeping! [22]

Do we really need all of this research to know that we are more energised and feel better when we have had enough sleep? Probably not.

If you want the energy that is going to fuel you towards a life of freedom, and which will give you quality hours rather than simply quantity, put your intuitive knowing about your sleep into practice and get the rest you need.

"There's practically no area of our lives that's not improved by getting adequate sleep."

– Arianna Huffington

Chapter summary

- No matter how passionate you are about something, you will eventually meet resistance because motivation, and even inspiration, will only take you so far. The only way we are going to be able to take on the force that is resistance is to generate greater levels of energy within ourselves.

- Your freedom lies in going after and achieving your dreams. You will need to manage your energy levels in order to keep pursuing your passions.

- Energy is your most valuable resource. It's more valuable than time because your energy levels determine how you spend your time.

- You can influence your energy levels – this is good news.

- There are two types of energy: body energy and mind energy. These energies influence each other: Exhausting one will exhaust the other, and recharging one will recharge the other.

- Your thoughts have a significant effect on your overall energy levels. Releasing worry and guilt (the wilt thought patterns), finding a sense of **meaning** or purpose, asking for help and meditation can all improve your thoughts and energy levels.

- On a physical level, engaging in regular exercise, eating a healthy diet, drinking plenty of water and getting enough sleep all contribute to your mind and body feeling energised.

Imagine all the ways your external world would transform if you lived with greater clarity about who you are and what you want for your life.

ELEMENT 5:

CALM

There's a voice in your mind that always has an opinion. It's always got something to say about what you're doing, what you did or what you should be doing. It has opinions about others and what they should be doing. It's always there; chattering away.

The voice is part of being human.

You know that voice in your mind, don't you?

If you're thinking: "*What voice? I don't have a voice in my mind.*"

That's the voice.

It might start saying something like:

I really need to get out for some exercise. I've put on weight and half my clothes don't fit me. I should eat better and exercise more. I'll exercise tonight. I'll go for a run. I wonder how many evenings per week I could fit in a run. I wonder if one of my girlfriends would be interested in joining me. I'll ask Sarah and Clare. It'll be more fun and I'll probably run further if I have a friend with me. But even if I can't find a friend, I still need to commit to regular exercise. It's healthy and I want to set a good example for the kids. Maybe the kids would like to join me. No, they'll probably just slow me down. I'll wait until their father gets home and then head out for some exercise...

The voice just keeps going if you let it. It has the capacity for a never ending stream of chatter. Mostly the chatter is a distraction from the present moment and it is rarely appeased. Even if you go out for exercise that evening, it will start up again:

Should I have stayed home to help Sam with his homework? He is struggling with maths. I'll make sure I check on him when I get back from my run. And I better make sure he has clean clothes for tomorrow. Maybe I don't have time to run for an hour tonight. I'll just run for half an hour so I'm not back too late. Why is there never enough time to get everything done? I don't understand how the other parents seem to be on top of everything and they have time to go to the gym. Perhaps I should ask Peter to help me. But he seemed so stressed when he was leaving for work this morning. What is going on with him? Maybe it's that new manager at his work. I suppose I'm lucky that my manager and I get along so well...

Occasionally the voice says things of substance and insight, but those thoughts are only a small portion of the continuous stream of chatter.

You might have noticed that the voice is never satisfied. No matter what you do. Almost as soon as you follow once piece of advice, the voice is telling you something completely different. Like when it says:

I really should give that guy a call back. I had a nice time on our date and he said he'd like to see me again. I might not feel that attracted to him now, but lots of people aren't that attracted when they first meet, then some of them end up getting married. I should just call him.

So you call him back, arrange another date and almost as soon as you hang up the phone, the voice starts again:

What did I do that for? This guy is really not my type. I should just wait until I meet someone that seems more my type. But I can't cancel now. Or maybe I can. I mean, I really don't want to waste his time if I don't think I'm interested in him...

The voice provides you with a constant monologue throughout the day. It doesn't really care which side of the argument it's on or whether it's being contradictory; it just likes to provide you with a never-ending stream of opinions, thoughts and judgements.

How do you tolerate the incessant chatter?

It's the thing keeping you awake on those nights you can't sleep. It's also getting in the way of you enjoying a sense of freedom.

What would it be like if you could turn the chatter off? It might be something like the experience described by Dr Jill Bolte Taylor in her 2008 TED talk.[23] She had had a stroke several years earlier, causing the left part of her brain to temporarily shut down and, along with it, the internal chatter.

According to Taylor, a neuroanatomist, the left hemisphere thinks linearly and methodically. It thinks in language. It generates the constant brain chatter, connecting your internal world to your external world. In the moment that Taylor lost the function of that part of her brain, there was total silence. At first this was shocking, but then she became captivated by the magnificence of the energy all around her. Dr Taylor described this experience as beautiful and joked that she was suddenly free of thirty-seven years of emotional baggage! All stress was gone and she felt euphoric. She felt she had been liberated and her spirit soared free. It was, she said, Nirvana.

However, Dr Taylor's experience also provides insight about the necessity of those parts of her brain that shut down. Sure, it was blissful when her brain went silent, but with half of her brain shut down, Dr Taylor could barely function in the physical world. She couldn't understand numbers, she couldn't speak properly and when people spoke to her, she didn't understand what they were saying. So the solution to all the chatter is not that you need to shut down the left half of your brain. Besides, there are plenty of cases where brains can still function – and still have chatter – with whole parts missing. The plasticity of the brain means that it can often adapt.

You need to do something about the internal chatter, though, if you want to experience freedom. Your most authentic and free self is underneath all the chatter. You know this because whenever you manage a quiet, peaceful moment, your free self speaks to you. Sometimes you call it intuition. It speaks your truth. And doesn't it sound different from the chatter? The voice of your free self is more like a whisper – sometimes a simple knowing that seems to have no sound at all.

Your free self wants you to grow and live your potential, so it often calls you to do things you're afraid of or have no skills at. When you listen, you hear it say, *'Keep going. You can do it. You can survive the pain associated with growth. You can succeed.'* Sometimes it tells you, *'Let go. You don't need that in your life anymore. You will be okay in spite of the loss. You can set yourself free.'*

Well, no wonder your chatter is drowning out your free self! The chatter is more about keeping you safe than taking risks. The chatter is often a reflection of the outdated map we discussed in the **self-knowledge** chapter. It's a reminder of when you were dependent on others and unable to look after yourself. It's connected to the fear of being wrong and leaves you constantly second guessing yourself... *Should I go out for exercise? Should I be at home with the kids? Should I call him? Should I move on? Should I speak my mind? Should I keep quiet? Should I follow my heart? Should I stay where it's safe?*

There is no right answer to any of these kinds of questions. The only thing you can really count on is that if you keep giving all your attention to the chatter, you'll go round and round in circles, usually in survival mode and on the lookout for danger. It's a recipe for a constant state of low-grade misery which will have you incessantly striving for ways to compensate for feeling disconnected from your most authentic and free self.

There is no real sense of freedom with the internal voice constantly chattering away. While you won't ever shut it off completely, just knowing you have the ability to generate the calm that comes from quieting the chatter will enhance your freedom.

"If you get the inside right, the outside will fall into place."

– Eckhart Tolle

The benefits of calm

Here are just some of the benefits of creating a calm mind:

- **Clarity.** With calm, you experience clarity about who you are and what you want for your life. You have clarity about how you are **responsible** for and contribute to what you are creating in your life, and insight into what you need to do to change your results.

- **Empathy and compassion.** In a space of calm, you are aware of your authentic self and give compassion to its vulnerability. This also leads to empathy for the humanity of others.

- **Love.** In calm, there is love. Feelings such as fear, hatred, envy or anger exist in the chatter. When the chatter is gone, so too are these feelings. But the feeling of love doesn't go anywhere; it is ever present – especially in the calm.

- **Confidence and courage.** So often, it's the chatter that prevents you from moving forward and taking action. With calm, you can hear your inner wisdom reminding you of how strong and capable you are, and how you can handle whatever challenges arise. With calm, you can find the courage to let go of old habits and beliefs, especially those that disempower you. In a place of calm, you realise that all the courage you need is already within you.

- **Insight and creativity.** Free from all the chatter, your mind is most available to hear your creative ideas and insights into how to handle certain situations, which you haven't been able to see before. It's often experienced as an 'a-ha' moment.

"Calm mind brings inner strength and self-confidence."

– Dalai Lama

Using calm to transform your external world

When you regularly cultivate a calm mind, the benefits discussed above become tools you can take into your external world. And don't we all need that? We live in a world where we are continuously fed the message that to be happy we need to source things from the external world. Like programmed robots, we constantly reach for our phones and other devices, only to find a never-ending stream of social media presenting a largely one-sided view. People on social media tend to share positive experiences much more than their challenges, mistakes or failures. This external chatter further fuels our internal chatter.

Allow yourself a moment right now to let go of all the chatter and fearful thoughts. If you're struggling to do this, tell yourself it's just for a moment so you can experiment.

Great, now let go and imagine all the ways your external world would transform if you lived with greater clarity about who you are and what you want for your life. Imagine how your relationships would expand and improve if you treated yourself and others with love and compassion. Imagine if you lived with confidence and had the **courage** to follow the inner wisdom you hear in the space of calm. And imagine if your creativity and insights were being channelled to you on a stronger signal so you could hear them more easily. How would your life transform? How free would you be?

All that you desire is available to you when you begin connecting regularly to a calm mind. As you generate calm and its benefits on an ongoing basis, these benefits also manifest in your external world. It's not always easy or effortless, but creating calm also creates strength and willpower. It takes strength and willpower to master your mind, silence your fears and create calm – but if you can master your mind, you can master your life.

> *"Panic causes tunnel vision. Calm acceptance of danger allows us to more easily assess the situation and see the options."*
>
> **– Simon Sinek**

Creating calm

I wasn't joking when I said it takes strength and willpower to create calm in your mind. Kicking the habit of excessive internal chatter is like kicking any ingrained habit – really challenging.

Like most people, I unintentionally had decades of practice at un- controlled chatter. After so many years of practice, it felt natural for my internal world to sometimes become so out of control and loud that it could drive to distraction. Life like that is not freedom! It is a form of self-torture.

Why do you put up with the internal chatter? One reason is that it's a way of keeping you safe. The chatter prevents you from going out and taking the risks that will ultimately set you free. But it also keeps you small. Another reason is it's a habit. Plain and simple, we create so much internal chatter because we are in the habit of it. We let the chatter get out of control, because we are not practiced at turning it off.

If you want freedom, it's time to create a new habit.

Meditation

One of the most well-known practices for creating calm, and something I highly recommend, is meditation. Meditation is about creating a calm mind so that with regular practice you can experience the benefits of calm.

There is a lot of information available about how to mediate. If you have never meditated, here are the basics:

1. Sit in a comfortable position with your spine upright.

2. Select a set period of time – fifteen to twenty minutes is good for beginners. Setting an alarm can be very helpful to free you from wondering how long you have been meditating. A set timeframe will encourage you to keep going when it's challenging, until the time is up.

3. Close your eyes. Breathe. Focus on your breath.

4. Keep focusing on your breath.

5. When thoughts come to mind, rather than give attention to them, simply notice them and let them go. If you realise your mind has started to wander, simply let that train of thought go and return your mind to focusing on your breath.

6. Any time you notice sounds, feelings, emotions or any other sensations, just acknowledge them and return your mind to your breath.

Ideally you will make meditation a regular part of your daily routine. But many people find it challenging to take time out of their day to simply meditate. It can feel impossible for people who are not practiced at it and can't imagine stopping all their busyness to simply sit with a quiet mind for a while.

I know that feeling. Here's how I got over it:

I practised meditation twice a day for forty-eight days straight. This idea was suggested by Wayne Dyer when I attended one of his workshops. I jumped at the idea, confident of how spiritual I would be during and after the forty-eight days. However, within the first few days, I hit resistance. I confirmed what I already thought to be true: I'm not good at meditation. I found my mind hardly cleared at all and spent most of the time thinking about random things that came to mind or worrying about things needed to be done. If Wayne hadn't said, "If you miss a day, you start again at Day 1," I probably would have started skipping sessions.

I persevered and the results were powerful and life changing. Most meditation sessions were fifteen to twenty minutes. When a session was going well, I would often choose to stay in meditation longer. I have never known peace like I did in those moments. Sometimes it felt like the whole world disappeared, yet I was connected to everything. Occasionally I saw colours, sometimes by choice and other times spontaneously. Any answers I needed for my life were accessible to me in those meditations. Fear evaporated. It was bliss and I wanted to stay in that state. When I eventually went to my calendar to check what day I was up to, I discovered I had been doing the meditation twice per day for fifty-three days!

If I hadn't committed, and continued to commit even when it was challenging, I never would have experienced the extraordinary. Those moments of bliss created a lifelong commitment to meditation because I now understand what's possible and how much of a difference the calm makes to my life and my sense of freedom.

Commit to meditating every day for a pre-determined period. Twice per day for forty-eight days is an excellent idea. At a minimum, commit to once per day.

After a forty-eight-day commitment, meditation will likely form part of your everyday life. From this place of understanding the benefits of meditation, you can move to what I refer to as 'flexible committed engagement'. This is when your practice is essential to your life and you're committed to keeping it that way, but you do not need to be as strict about it (so you don't need to include a rule such as 'if you miss a day, you start again at Day 1').

I aim to meditate every day. However, if I meditate six days in a week, I feel I am doing very well. My experience is that the positive effects of six days a week have a lingering effect that lasts past the day I missed.

If I start missing days more often, I know I am much more likely to succumb to all the noise, busyness and resistance that will ultimately slow me down – the exact opposite of what I'm attempting to do. By that, I mean I am attempting to be my most effective and productive while also being happy. Getting caught up in everyday busyness and chatter will make me less productive, effective and happy.

It can be tempting to stop meditating when things are going well. It's important to keep going. The good habits and strength gained through your regular practice will help you when life is more challenging. Don't wait for life to get challenging – which it inevitably will.

"I practice staying calm all the time, beginning with situations that aren't tense."

– Martha Beck

Even if you struggle to meditate six or three or fewer days a week, don't give up entirely. Do as much as you can. Do whatever you can to build the habit of calm. You will still gain benefits for the time you put into creating a calm mind. As Sam Harris said in his book *Waking Up*,[24] "We need not become masters of meditation to realize its benefits."

Calm commitment

I would like to say a bit more about 'flexible committed engagement' – which I also refer to as 'calm commitment'. This is when you are fully committed to your practice and take action accordingly, but are relaxed about it. To be stressed about it would completely undo what you are creating with your meditation practice. If you notice yourself becoming frustrated or stressed about not keeping to your commitment, just simply notice and then take action to correct it. Just like when you are distracted during meditation, you simply take notice and then return your attention to your breath. When you notice you have become distracted from your commitment to your practice, you can simply notice and correct.

One of my role models for calm commitment is Pema Chodron. She often says things that make me smile and remind me to surrender to the process. In an audio recording I have of a conversation between Pema Chodron and Alice Walker,[25] Walker described how she was meditating very regularly for about a year and then just stopped. She wondered why this had happened and asked Pema, "Does this ever happen to you?" Pema responded, "Yes, and I don't worry about it."

She doesn't worry about it! Pema, while very committed to her spiritual journey, seems to have a wonderful level of flexibility and freedom around her practice. She understands and expresses that if you're feeling stressed or critical about your practice, then you're missing the point of the practice.

> *A student went to his meditation teacher and*
> *said, "My meditation is horrible! I feel so distracted,*
> *or my legs ache, or I'm constantly falling asleep. It's*
> *just horrible!"*
> *"It will pass," the teacher said matter-of-factly.*
> *A week later, the student came back to his*
> *teacher. "My meditation is wonderful! I feel so aware,*
> *so peaceful, so alive! It's just wonderful!'*
> *"It will pass," the teacher replied matter-of-factly.*

Other ways to create calm

While meditation is one of the most powerful ways to create calm, it is not the only way.

A suitable practice for creating calm could be anything that quiets all the chatter of your mind and, instead, engages you with the present. Whatever it is for you, it will likely be something that you feel passionate about. Passion causes you to feel inspired to better yourself, to push through resistance and to rise above unnecessary dramas.

Activities that can create calm include:

- **Writing** – Whenever I was focused on writing this book, I felt calm.

- **Yoga** – Yoga encourages focus on the different poses and being present.

- **Painting** – Many artists describe the calm they experience while painting.

- **Reading** – This is especially the case with books that inspire you, including spiritual texts.

- **Running** – A good friend of mine describes her running practice as a form of meditation.

- **Sport** – This could be a team or an individual sport, any sport in which you love to participate.

- **Dancing** – The movement of dancing can create awareness of the body and bring you into the present moment.

- **Playing music or singing** – These can also bring your attention into the present.

- **Cooking** – Many people are passionate about food and flavours, and eating!

- **Walking** – The poet Wallace Stevens said, "Perhaps all truth depends on a walk around the lake." As a keen walker, I wholeheartedly agree.

This is just a short list of ways to create a calm mind. The possibilities are endless, though, because you can choose anything that causes you to be present.

More freedom thoughts (author's favourites)

Further to the freedom thoughts listed in the meaning chapter, here are some more of my favourites. These have served me well for enhancing my sense of calm.

Whenever I notice a lot of chatter, I usually find myself repeating whichever one is most appropriate. Sometimes the reminder is all I need in order to just let go of all the noise, and be present. At a minimum, the reminder always seems to make life easier.

Again, if you think they could be useful, I suggest keeping a copy of them where you will be reminded in times of challenge.

'Before enlightenment, chop wood, carry water. After enlightenment, chop wood, carry water.'

I used to think that once I reached some higher level of awareness or education or enlightenment, I would no longer be plagued by some of what I perceived to be the mundane or frustrating aspects of life. This proverb reminds me that life and all it entails still happens, but I can choose the state of mind I want to be in throughout it all.

'Give so much time to the improvement of yourself that you don't have time to criticise others.'

This Jim Rohn quote was written on my whiteboard for more than a year. The regular reminder totally changed the results I was getting and the amount of frustration I felt about things that other people did. I significantly reduced the amount of time I spent being critical of other people. Any time I noticed myself feeling critical of what someone else did, I would say to myself, *'Clearly you have some spare time if you have time to be critical of others. Perhaps you could put that time into something more productive.'* Half of this book was written on the back of the annoying things that other people did. It eventually got to the point where I began to appreciate it when I felt annoyed by other people because I learnt how to turn the negative energy into something positive.

'It's a first world problem.'

I'm almost embarrassed to say that it sometimes feels like a chore to go out and get lunch. Or it's sometimes frustrating that I need to put petrol in the car. Or that I need to get my hair cut. None of these or any of the myriad of activities like them should be given negative meanings that drain energy. They are, in fact, excellent opportunities to be grateful for all that we have in our first-world lives.

'Let it go if you want to be free.'

Sometimes, when I am struggling to forgive someone, I reflect on Nelson Mandela and attempt to channel even a hundredth of the strength, humility, love and discipline he possessed. I mean, how does someone emerge from prison after twenty-seven years without any bitterness or anger? When he was asked this question, he responded, "Yes, I was angry. And I was a little afraid. After all, I'd not been free in so long. But when I felt that anger well up inside of me I realised that if I hated them after I got outside that gate then they would still have me. I wanted to be free so I let it go." His words remind me that when I choose to forgive others,

I don't need to do it for them, and it does not mean that what happened in the past is okay. I forgive in order to set myself free.

'Pain is inevitable. Suffering is a choice.'

Whether it's physical or emotional, pain is a natural part of life that can't be avoided. I do have control over how much I suffer though. I can take **responsibility** for how I have contributed to my pain. I can be selective about the **meanings** I attach to the causes of my pain. And I can practise **calm**.

'What's your hurry?'

I often encounter clients who are caught up in the sense that they are running out of time. I can empathise because I sometimes get a scarcity mentality around time too. The scarcity mentality is not useful. It's a fight with reality that creates busyness rather than effectiveness. Yes, life is short, but 'hurry' is not helpful. It often lacks focus. I can actually make better decisions, be more effective and get more done when I choose calm and remind myself to be more present.

Chapter summary

- The ongoing chatter in your mind is a barrier to experiencing freedom. You need to create calm in your mind.

- The benefits of calm include clarity, empathy and compassion, love, confidence and courage, insight and creativity.

- Excessive disempowering internal chatter is a habit. You can choose to create a new habit.

- As you generate calm and its benefits on an ongoing basis, these benefits manifest in your external world. It's not always easy or effortless, but it is worth it for the strength and willpower that creating calm generates.

- Meditation is one of the most well-known practices for creating calm. Ideally, you will incorporate meditation as a regular part of your daily routine.

- It is recommended that you commit to practice meditation for a set period (e.g. twice a day for forty-eight days) as a way to gain true experience with meditation and to create a habit.

- We need not become masters of meditation to realise its benefits.

- Calm commitment is more effective than worrying about your meditation practice.

- Other ways to create calm include activities you enjoy, such as: writing, yoga, painting, reading, dancing, music, cooking or any sport you enjoy.

*When you are responsible,
you understand that you
have power over how you
experience everything
in your life.*

ELEMENT 6:

RESPONSIBILITY

My client Lenica recently left her job because one of the managers at her workplace treated her disrespectfully and regularly put her down. As she complained during one of our coaching sessions, it was obvious she felt a lot of anger and resentment toward her former manager.

This resentment caused Lenica to feel stressed throughout the day and to lose sleep at night, which indicated that she was still quite emotionally attached to the situation. Strong emotion is often a sign that our issues are more about ourselves than the people or circumstances we are blaming. In Lenica's case, the real issue was more that she had let herself down than someone else had wronged her. But it can be challenging to turn the mirror on ourselves and admit that. Instead we tend to direct blame at others, often unconsciously.

It seemed apparent to me that Lenica had fallen into this trap of blaming others. I knew this was a disempowering position to put herself in so I asked her, "What is it about you that sends the message 'put me down' to your manager?" I could tell by Lenica's silence and the look on her face that she felt torn. Part of her wanted to keep making her manager wrong for putting her down constantly. Another part of her wanted to uncover and deal with the real issue so that she didn't have to keep encountering it in her life.

Out of the silence, Lenica chose to evolve. She began listing all the ways that she was sending the message to her manager and other people in her life that it was acceptable to put her down. For example, Lenica admitted that she often acted in a passive-aggressive way rather than speaking assertively about her concerns when they arose. And while she already knew she did this sometimes, she'd never really taken the time to connect the pieces and see how this kind of behaviour was contributing to her reality. As she began taking responsibility for her role in the situation, Lenica could see that her pain did not come from others putting her down as much as it did from the way she let herself down.

In the moment she took responsibility, everything shifted. Lenica had a new level of clarity about her power to create situations in her life. She could also see that she would not be empowered or feel free as long as she was not taking responsibility for the role she played.

Like Lenica, you teach people how to treat you. You can take responsibility for that. You can choose to step into your power and send a new message to those around you. If another person isn't empathetic or open to adjusting how they treat you, you can ask yourself: "Am I communicating my message in such a way that it will be received and respected by the other person?"

If you believe you have been respectful and clear but your message has been disregarded, you then have another choice: Accept the behaviour of the other person or leave. If you choose to accept the behaviour, you do so knowing that you've made a conscious choice and you won't hold onto resentment. If you decide to leave, you do so knowing that you chose to be assertive rather than be a victim. Whatever you decide to do, do it without giving your power away by telling yourself that external factors have control over how you experience your life.

Responsibility means understanding that you have created or, at a minimum, co-created your experience of life. While there will always be some things outside your control, you understand that you have control over how you respond to people or events.

Responsibility is your superpower

When I truly understood the concept of being responsible, I had visions of being Superwoman, super cape and all! Seriously, understanding what it really meant to take responsibility had a profound impact on my experience and my power to create my life. That feeling of power had me envisioning myself in a superhero outfit, the letter 'R' for Responsibility emblazoned across my puffed-up chest, standing with my hands on my hips and feeling totally assured of my ability to achieve anything.

Sound ridiculous?

It's nowhere near as ridiculous as giving your power away and leaving it up to external factors to write your destiny and create your reality.

The fact is that when you are responsible, you understand that you have power over how you experience everything in your life.

When you choose to be responsible for all that you create and experience in your life, you can expect:

- To feel empowered – You'll tap into your superpower as the co-creator of your life.

- Catharsis – Taking responsibility means letting go of any guilt or hurt associated with any mistakes or regrets of the past.

- A more creative mind – A mind that takes responsibility is primed for creating solutions and ideas.

- To be inspiring to others – Your **courage** to take responsibility will give others courage to do the same.

- **Courage** – Each time you take responsibility, you discover that what follows is rarely as bad as you feared. In other words, the repercussions of taking responsibility aren't nearly as scary as you imagine them to be. Each time you take action and reinforce this truth, you build the courage to continue being responsible.

Why do we avoid responsibility?

In spite of the power and freedom that comes from taking responsibility for yourself and your life, many people avoid it. Why?

Fear. People usually associate being responsible with the fear of being blamed if something goes wrong.

We prefer to be right and have the approval of others because it makes us feel safe. By avoiding responsibility, we have a free pass from blame. If something goes wrong, we can use phrases such as: 'It's not my fault,' or 'It wasn't my idea,' or 'Don't look at me, I'm not in charge.' This is often not an easy mindset to break away from. Society and our culture do not often afford us the option to fail, and the judgements around failure are rife.

We have learned that it's safer to give responsibility over to our employers, spouses, adult children, financial advisors or the government. Unfortunately, it happens sometimes that the person or entity to whom we are handing responsibility is also giving the responsibility over to someone else. In the event that something goes wrong, few people are willing to put their hand up to own the results.

It's not surprising that we usually stick to the status quo, keep our lives small and blame others when things go wrong. This is why it is so powerful and inspiring when someone takes a risk and succeeds – because we instinctively know they had to go up against the risk of ridicule. These people are symbols of inspiration and **courage** because the great majority of us play small and won't risk ridicule.

Perhaps you gain a perception of safety by avoiding responsibility, but at what cost?

It comes at the cost of your freedom.

It is inevitable that you will make mistakes. Personal freedom means having the freedom to be wrong and to accept the responsibility and pain that goes with being wrong without falling apart.

"The difficulty we have in accepting responsibility for our behaviour lies in the desire to avoid the pain of the consequences of that behaviour. Whenever we seek to avoid the responsibility for our own behaviour, we do so by attempting to give that responsibility to some other individual or organisation or entity. But this means we then give away our power to that entity."

– M. Scott Peck

"Can freedom become a burden, too heavy for man to bear, something he tries to escape from? Is there not also, perhaps, besides an innate desire for freedom, an instinctive wish for submission?"

– Erich Fromm

When should we start taking responsibility?

It's probably not reasonable to say to a young child, "you have con- trol over how you respond to anything that happens in your life" or "you are the co-creator of your reality". I don't recommend putting un- reasonable expectations on children about how they deal with events and corresponding emotions. Children's brains are still developing and, fortunately, most of us accept that while it's not necessarily a nice experience, it's quite normal for children to yell or have tantrums if life doesn't go the way they want.

This kind of behaviour doesn't help us as adults. We've all witnessed an adult losing their temper and it's not pretty. I remember in my early twenties, my boyfriend at the time lost his temper. I assume he was annoyed at me for something I did, but I don't recall what it was that upset him so much. What I do remember is that he took off the new trainers I bought him for his birthday and threw them on the roof of his house! Looking back, I find it a little humorous and ridiculous, but at the time, I think I was more stunned and frightened.

In that moment, it was like he reverted to being a toddler. Throwing things like he did is quite normal for a young child. Looking back, I can see his behaviour provided an outlet for thoughts and emotions he hadn't yet learned to control. And he likely got some short term satis- faction from intimidating those around him. But in the long term, if he was willing to reflect on his behaviour, he would have to admit that he acted like a spoilt child. What I know to be true though, is he was behaving in the best way he knew how and in alignment with what he'd learned throughout his life.

We've probably all behaved like spoilt children when we've been old enough to know better. Perhaps you deliberately broke something, lied, called a friend or colleague names, or blamed someone for a mistake that wasn't entirely their fault. When we behave in these ways, the amount of pain we experience is often linked to the extent to which we knew we could or should have handled the situation better; when we say to ourselves *"Why did I do that? I know I am capable of better than this."*

We can't necessarily expect better from children because their brains are still developing. As adults, however, we are capable of better. But capable doesn't necessarily mean that we have learned how to do it well. When I think about that ex-boyfriend, who was well into his twenties, he had never learned to pause when he felt angry or upset, or to ask himself, "How have I contributed to this situation?" or at least "What could I do to make myself feel better than doesn't involve intimidating other people or behaving like a child?" He just never learned how to do that.

Becoming an adult doesn't mean you automatically become responsible. In many countries, you are considered an adult around age eighteen to twenty-one. Overnight, simply because you had a birthday, you are allowed to vote and drink alcohol. There is no test to confirm whether you can do either of these things well; they're just given to you. Mess up and you are also at risk of jail because you're now old enough for that too.

Is it reasonable to expect that someone knows how to be responsible by the time they are legally an adult?

It depends on how you define 'being responsible'. If we define 'being responsible' as knowing right from wrong, then yes, they are old enough to be responsible.

But what about being responsible in a way that enhances our freedom? What about taking full responsibility for who we are and for our experience of the world – rather than believing the world owes us something?

While this form of responsibility has little to do with age, most people have not learned this skill by the time they are legally an adult (yes, responsibility is a skill that can be learned). Many don't learn it until decades later and some never do. It is certainly unreasonable to expect, if you were never taught how, that you will turn eighteen and overnight begin taking responsibility for how you experience life. You won't suddenly be aware that making others responsible for what happens in your life comes at the cost of your own empowerment, freedom and control over your destiny.

So when should we have learned to take on this responsibility? For the sake of putting a number on it, I suggest that we should have learned to take on this responsibility by the age of twenty-five or thirty at the latest. Ideally, you would have learned to have a mindset of responsibility even earlier.

Was I taking full responsibility for how I experienced my life by the time I was twenty-five?

No.

You might say I was responsible by social standards by the time I was twenty-five. I was financially independent by my early twenties, left home at twenty-one and have always had a job or run my own business. I bought a house and put myself through university. But I did all of it without any true sense of freedom. In fact, most of what I achieved by that age was largely out of fear of doing the wrong thing and a scarcity mindset.

I didn't even have a mindset of full responsibility by the time I was thirty. I was too fearful, too low on self-esteem and I regularly looked for ways to make others responsible for my outcomes. However, I believe I would have been capable of being fully responsible by that age if I'd had helpful tools earlier in life, such as this book or a mentor. I was old enough to understand what it meant to be fully responsible and to put those insights into action. I just didn't know what I didn't know.

If you are a bit (or a lot) older than twenty-five and the concept of full responsibility is a revelation, don't waste time regretting what you didn't know before now.

Overall, society and mainstream media don't educate us about how to be fully responsible for all that happens in our lives. We are not educated about how liberating it is to decide that 'taking responsibility is self-empowering' or 'I create my experiences.' Instead, we regularly see examples on TV and in the media of people attempting to avoid blame, even when they are clearly at fault. And marketers aren't interested in us taking full responsibility for our lives. They want us to think we'll be happy if we purchase their products.

We experience all this from a young age. If we start to question what we have been taught, we usually only begin doing so in adolescence. By the time you reach your late teens, you are only just beginning to embark on the possibility of 'unlearning' everything you have been taught, but which you suspect is not serving you or helping you create the life you want. If you're lucky, during this important life stage you have people around you who inspire, empower and challenge you in healthy ways.

This is a stage where you have the mental capacity to write the rules for your life and achieve a level of independence that enables you to follow through with those rules. Perhaps it is fortunate that society now allows more time for this period of transition and self-discovery. People are marrying and having children later and higher education is much more common than it was a couple of decades ago.

Through his extensive research of young people in Western culture around the ages of eighteen to twenty-five, Jeffrey Jensen Arnett has learned a great deal about how they experience and perceive the world and their place in it. Something common to them is that they definitely do not consider themselves teenagers, but they also do not yet consider themselves adults. Arnett has labelled this cohort 'emerging adults'.

He says the time of being an emerging adult:

> '... is when most people begin to move toward making the commitments that structure adult life: marriage (or a long-term partnership), parenthood, and a long-term job. I sometimes use eighteen to twenty-five to refer to emerging adulthood and sometimes eighteen to twenty-nine, because the end of it is highly variable. Nothing magical happens at age twenty-five

to end it. For most people the late twenties are a time of moving toward a more settled adult life, but there are many, especially the highly educated urban young, who continue their emerging adult lifestyle through their late twenties and into their early thirties.'[26]

By the age of thirty, many people have achieved or are actively working on achieving all of the usual trappings that go along with being an adult, such as a career or business, marriage, children who are well looked after, a nice car and a vacation every year. Their experience of themselves, however, usually doesn't align with what they believe it means to be an adult. More often, they feel like they are an imposter inadequately filling the role – and they continue to feel this way until they update their map (***self-knowledge***), improve their ***self-worth*** and take responsibility for all they are creating in their life and the world. I see this regularly with clients who are in their thirties, forties or older and have still not adopted a mindset of responsibility. They feel trapped within a self-created prison. Thankfully, it doesn't have to be that way.

Responsibility always starts now

If you're thinking that you've been lacking a mindset of responsibility, ensure you don't waste any time beating yourself up about it. Let go of the past. Responsibility starts now. Saying anything less is to abdicate responsibility in the present moment; there is no freedom in regret.

If you're like me and didn't learn what it means to be fully responsible or truly free until you were in your thirties or even older, don't concern yourself with any ideas about having wasted time in the wrong mindset. It is pointless to compare yourself to others who had a different journey from you. Simply start your journey from wherever you are. While it might have been great to learn how to have a mindset of responsibility a decade earlier, I'm grateful I learned it when I did and not a decade later.

Today is always an opportunity to let go, move on, embrace your power and be the creator of how you experience your reality. You have all that you need – a mind that can create your entire world. And it does. Your mind has played a role in your history and it will determine your future. It co-creates every relationship you have.

If you want your freedom, start taking responsibility now. The second you take ownership of your life, past and present, you create a world of new possibilities.

Creating responsibility

Will you be at the whim of external forces, or will you see the ways you have co-created your life?

Being responsible might sound easy in theory, however, it's rarely easy in practice because we usually have to unlearn some old ways of thinking. But it is possible and rewarding. Here are four powerful strategies to assist you in adopting a mindset of responsibility.

Understand the responsibility spectrum

There will always be some things outside of your control. You share this planet and your life with other people and you do not have control over what others they do. Influence, at best, is all you have.

So how do you know when to take responsibility and when to hold others accountable for their contribution to your reality?

This is important because taking responsibility for things that are not your fault can be just as detrimental to your freedom as not taking enough responsibility.

At the same time, understanding what you are and are not responsible for is one of your greatest challenges. A life of freedom includes understanding and accepting that every day is a never-ending process of assessing where your responsibilities lie.

Therapist and author M. Scott Peck shared how most of the clients who came to him for help were dealing with either a neurosis or a character disorder. Dr Peck argued that both types of cases were disorders of responsibility and, as such, opposite styles of relating to the world and its problems. The neurotic assumes too much responsibility; when they encounter challenges they assume they are at fault. Someone with a character disorder assumes the world is at fault.[7] Those of us who are not at either end of that spectrum will be constantly navigating the terrain in between.

Your never-ending navigation of the responsibility spectrum will become easier when you strengthen your other freedom elements. For example, it takes **self-knowledge** to understand yourself and the strategies you have adopted to avoid taking responsibility. If you look closely at yourself, perhaps you'll discover you are in the habit of 'playing the victim'. And you might find you get a certain payoff, such as attention and sympathy from others, when you're a victim of your circumstances rather than responsible. **Self-worth** and **courage** are also helpful when you want to be responsible. If you are weak on these elements, you're more likely to fear failure and blame if something goes wrong, and therefore prone to letting others assume responsibility.

So, first, understand that there is a responsibility spectrum that you and everyone needs to navigate. Then, take the journey of this spectrum with curiosity and a view that responsibility is your superpower for creating how you experience life.

Stop blaming your parents

Once while on a train, a friend explained how his current issues were because he was an only child. I thought about that for a moment and then said, "Well, you were an only child. Now you're an only adult." In other words, it was time for him to stop using his childhood experiences as excuses for why he did the ineffective things he did.

He wasn't alone – I also used my childhood experiences to excuse my behaviour.

For years I believed my parents stuffed me up. I thought they really did a number on me. It seemed clear they preferred my younger brother, even though he was a problem child. They didn't have much time or energy to give to me after dealing with his issues. In my view at the time, they weren't cool, they didn't understand me, they didn't teach me confidence or self-worth or how to experience my emotions. Instead, I absorbed a lot of insecurities and shame, and the way I treated myself and allowed others to treat me reflected that.

How did that paragraph make you feel? Did it resonate with you, making you think, *'Yeah, sounds like my childhood'?* Or perhaps you thought, *'Are you kidding? At least your parents were around. I haven't seen my dad since I was five years old,'* or *'Give me a break. My mother was an alcoholic and my father abused me,'* or *'My mother tried to commit suicide on the day I told her I wasn't putting up with her crap any more'.* Or maybe your experience was positive and you believe *'My parents did the best they knew how to do. They were excellent parents.'*

Nobody gets through childhood unscathed. We all get to the other side of childhood with wounds, no matter how well intentioned our parents were. You could say author and psychologist Oliver James is an expert on parenting, and even he expects to make mistakes with his own children. As written is his book *They F*** You Up,* "It is inevitable that even the best of parents will make mistakes."[27]

Everything I said about my parents can be true or not true, depending on how I look at it. It's possible my parents will read this book and be a little offended by the previous description. But what's also true is I have never once doubted my parents' love for me. They provided me with life's necessities, a good education and overseas travel experiences when I was a teenager (even though we were not wealthy). They instilled in me the values of respect and love. They taught me a good work ethic, finance and communication skills. Ultimately, they achieved what all parents want for their children: providing a better life than they had themselves. They did that and much more.

I've learned to have more appreciation and empathy for my parents but I first had to grow up mentally and emotionally to be able to do that. I really started to grow up when I realised that my parents were human, just like me, and I forgave them for that rather than holding it against them. My parents were just fumbling their way through life and they still are – just like me. For me to expect anything more from them is just a fight with reality that I am destined to lose. They are human – nothing more and nothing less. They are worthy of love and respect even though they will continue to make mistakes, grow and learn – just like me.

Now that I am endeavouring to live a life of freedom, none of the past experiences I recall about my parents, positive or negative, have any part to play in my ability to be responsible.

Remember, responsibility starts now. None of what happened in your past is a barrier to you creating a life of freedom in the present.

How is your relationship with your parents? Do you experience any of the following?

- You have unreasonable negative feelings towards your parents. For example, your negative feelings are more intense than you would feel towards a friend who had done the same things.

- You speak down to your parents or don't treat them with the same respect as you would a friend.

- You are estranged from your parents and are still angry at them. (If you're estranged from your parents but you have resolved the negative emotions and explored any ways in which you have contributed to the breakdown, then there is nothing inherently wrong with being estranged. Sometimes, unfortunately, it might be the healthiest option.) But if you don't know how to be with your parents because you still feel resentful and angry and haven't dealt with those emotions, that's another story.

- You try to punish, control or make your parents feel guilty for the ways you perceive they have wronged you (note: we sometimes aren't even aware when we do this).

If you do experience any of these, then you have some growing up to do before you can declare that you are being fully responsible for your life. Taking responsibility means no longer blaming your parents. It's saying to yourself, *'They got it wrong sometimes'*, and responding with, *'They did the best they knew how to. I'm an adult now. I have a wealth of knowledge at my disposal. I can take it from here.'* When you can say this with love and mean it, you are one giant step closer to claiming your freedom. It might not come easily; resolving the wounds of childhood rarely happens without a decent amount of self-exploration, enquiry and forgiveness.

Even when you get to that point, you can expect to regress sometimes. You might still have moments of feeling anger or resentment towards your parents, even if they are not alive any more. That's natural. The relationship you had as a child with your primary caregivers had a bigger influence on you than any other relationship ever could. Studies have shown this repeatedly. This is why we can't have a conversation about being fully responsible and creating a life of freedom without talking about your parents or other people who raised you.

We also can't have a conversation about any of the ways your parents might have wronged you without also having a conversation about how they served you. What are your biggest strengths? Are you fierce and independent? Are you loving? Successful? Talented? You are any and all of these things in some way and you owe that at least in part to those who raised you - even if they contributed to those qualities within you indirectly. Many people spend a greater part of their lives resenting what their parents did or didn't do without recognising that those experiences also positively shaped their gifts, attitudes and strengths. When we choose to be grateful for the hardships we've experienced, because of how they served us, then we are taking responsibility for who we are today.

The five per cent

I've done some foolish things in my life and it doesn't feel comfortable to admit that I was responsible for them. If I'm honest, I probably could have taken responsibility for them at the time. There's not a single foolish thing I've done in my adult life that I didn't at least suspect was foolish at the time. Sometimes I knew it beyond doubt but I didn't want to acknowledge it. Other times it was a subtle knowing, like a whisper in my mind that I could drown out with my own justifications or by rounding up the support from caring friends who were willing to listen to and support my stories.

I regularly see examples of others also avoiding responsibility. Clients rarely mean to be evasive – it is simply their humanity and outdated maps that causes them to be in denial instead of taking responsibility for the outcomes they are achieving.

While being fully responsible can be challenging, it is also our strongest point of power. So as a coach, I use the *Five Per cent Model* to help my clients find that point of power.

Sometimes a client will tell me about what's going on, what the outcomes are and all the ways in which it is the fault of [enter object of blame here]. It could be the workplace's fault, the boss's fault, the spouse's fault, the ex-spouse's fault, the parents' fault, society's fault or even a random stranger's fault. I listen respectfully, all the while noting the ways they are disempowering themselves. I often sense that my client is at least fifty per cent responsible for what has happened or how they are feeling (remember, we co-create our reality). Maybe even – dare I say it – 100 per cent responsible?

In that moment, my client very likely does not want to hear that they are 100 per cent or even fifty per cent responsible for the situation which has upset them. Many struggle with being even twenty per cent responsible – in that moment, anyway. I've learned that suggesting to a client that they are five per cent responsible doesn't encounter much resistance. So that's the number I usually go with, though the actual number doesn't really matter. I just need my client to focus on what they are doing (no matter how small) that is co-creating their reality, because that is where they have some control and the power to create change.

After I've heard their story, I draw a circle on the page and say, "Here is the situation." Then I draw a triangular slither in the circle, like a thin piece cut into a pie and say, "Let's say this slice represents the five per cent of this situation for which you are responsible. What is it that you are doing that constitutes that five per cent?"

In the moment that my client focuses on how they have contributed to the situation, they are in control. They are no longer a victim of their circumstances but a conscious, empowered participant in their lives.

You can do this too. Draw the circle on a piece of paper if it helps. No matter how much of your challenges you think are not your fault, you will at least be able to claim five per cent responsibility. Hone in on that five per cent. Get curious and wonder what else about this situation would change if you were to change that five per cent that you have control over. There is freedom in owning the five per cent.

Scheduled irresponsibility

Sometimes it really feels like it would be easier to blame others or circumstances for all the things in my life that I'm not happy about. It's an option. I do have that choice. I can either be 'at cause' (responsible) when it comes to how I experience life, or I can be 'at effect' (irresponsible) and think that life just happens to me and I have no control over it.

I like to believe I spend the great majority of my life from the viewpoint of being 'at cause'. Even so, there are times when *I JUST WANT A MOMENT TO BE COMPLETELY IRRESPONSIBLE.* These are times when I'm feeling a bit (or a lot) fed up or tired. Being responsible just feels a little too hard and I'd really just like to whinge about life instead.

If you ever feel like that too, I say don't fight it. It can actually be more productive to move through the feeling.

Here's how it works ...

First, you need a friend who also understands this exercise. I have a good friend who I chat with regularly. We tend to hold a similar perspective about life and the need to be at cause in our lives. We are also in agreement that sometimes it can be helpful to express feelings of irresponsibility, or, in other words, have a whinge!

I ask my friend: 'Permission to be at effect?'

Already knowing what I mean, she responds with: 'Permission granted.' With those words, she is signalling her understanding that I really want to get to a place of being responsible, but I first need to get some ineffective ways of thinking out of my system.

I then proceed to just vent all my unhelpful and unproductive thoughts, getting them out of my head via my mouth. I mean, I really let loose! The venting will probably include phrases like: 'I shouldn't have to do this,' or 'She did that to spite me,' or 'Why does he always have to do that?' or 'It's not fair,' or 'I'm tired of having to do that,' or 'Why does life have to be so difficult?' or [insert any one of a thousand possible complaints about your life].

All of these kinds of thoughts are unproductive and often not even true. The point of this exercise, however, is to let yourself be irrational. I've even gone so far as to complain, 'Why can't it just work out for once,' in relation to my life. Anyone who knows me knows how ridiculous that statement is and how much I love my life. But sometimes I just need a moment to acknowledge and vent about those parts of my life that don't seem to be working.

Choosing to be at effect in this way (i.e. choosing an appropriate time and asking a friend for permission, and, most importantly, acknowledging that you are *choosing* to be at effect) is actually a constructive way of shifting to a position of responsibility. If you have a whole lot of unproductive thoughts swimming around in your head, they can prevent you from moving forward. Having a 'permission to be at effect' session, however, can assist you in gaining clarity and motivation to take action, because at the end of your vent you are left with the simple truth that just whining and complaining about issues doesn't solve them.

Chapter summary

- You will not be empowered or free in your life until you are willing to take responsibility.

- Responsibility means understanding that you have created or, at a minimum, co-created all of your past, present and future experiences. While there will always be some things outside of your control, being responsible means you understand that you have control over how you respond and, therefore, your experience.

- Responsibility is your superpower!

- Many of us avoid responsibility because we associate being responsible with the fear of being blamed if something goes wrong. However, this attitude is disempowering and puts us in a victim mentality.

- Becoming an adult doesn't mean you automatically become responsible. There is some unlearning that needs to happen so you can let go of any fear associated with being fully responsible.

- Many of us blame our parents for the way we are and our experience of life. However, this pattern prevents us from taking responsibility for our lives.

- To truly stand in your power, it's important to actively take ownership of everything you can. The cost of avoiding responsibility is your freedom.

Never underestimate the value of the personal battles you chose to face and the courage it took to do so.

ELEMENT 7:

COURAGE

Courage is faith. It is your willingness to keep moving forward and taking on life, even when the outcome is uncertain. And the outcome is always uncertain.

This is why courage is the last element – because no matter how much you have prepared, no matter how much experience you have or how well you are living the other freedom elements, in the end all you can do is move forward in faith.

Your inner wisdom is constantly calling you to be one step ahead of where you are now. So it is always calling you into the unknown.

If you resist the call due to fear of the unknown or fear of failing, you are keeping yourself captive. Everything will be restricted. You won't love as much as you could. You won't speak your truth. You won't declare who you are to the world or to those you care most about. You won't live with freedom.

Without courage, you risk arriving at the end of your life with regrets, like so many who have left it too late to live a life of freedom. When Bronnie Ware nursed people who were dying, she heard the same regrets described over and over. She shared these regrets in her book, *The Top Five Regrets of the Dying*[28]. Her patients wished they'd had the courage to live a life true to themselves and not the life that others had expected of them. They wished they'd had the courage to express their feelings and to let themselves be happier. The questions Ware heard regularly from her terminally-ill patients were, "Why didn't I just do what I wanted?" and "Why wasn't I strong enough?"

It's not hard to imagine how someone gets to the end of their life with these kinds of regrets given that most of us experience them on a weekly basis.

What is it going to take for you to finally say, 'I will not go another week regretting that I didn't do what I know, in my Spirit, I should have done?'

When your mind is chattering away and telling you to hold off or stay back or quit, what's it going to take to keep your freedom and to keep moving forward to growth?

It's going to take faith that no matter what you decide to do, no matter what risks you take, it will all turn out okay.

And it will.

As stated in the most optimism-inducing quote (attributed to John Lennon) I've ever heard ...

> *"Everything will be okay in the end. If it's not okay, it's not the end."*

So whatever challenge you are going through right now, or whatever challenge you are thinking of taking on, keep going.

You need to keep moving forward in faith – and this takes courage.

Creating courage

We are often not as courageous as we could be because we undervalue what it means to be courageous. The common belief about courage is that it's an uncommon power. We rarely feel it within ourselves because we perceive courage to be something extraordinary. And we don't feel extraordinary.

Unfortunately, when we misdiagnose what it means to be courageous, we miss important opportunities to develop our own courage. Too often we view courage as the domain of exceptional beings with some kind of magical power. Our history and the media are filled with stories and myths about ancient gods, super heroes, wizards and the supernatural.

Don't get me wrong. I love these stories and what they represent. I was raised on Jedi Knights and I adore Harry Potter. I have a never-ending appreciation for the hero's journey, from calling, to resistance, to undertaking training, to the ultimate triumph over their enemies. These stories are a representation of the journey we all take if we choose to follow the calling of our spirits and claim our freedom.

Too often though, we close the book or the movie finishes and we are back in *real* life. We attempt to ignore the calling of our spirit because we think we don't have the superhero-like power it would take to deal with all the challenges along the way.

But neither did Luke Skywalker or Harry Potter or Wonder Woman. Not really. Because they aren't *real.*

They do, however, represent something very real – the possibilities that exist within every one of us.

We need to take the lessons of these wonderful, insightful stories and bring them into our lives. In the human realm, there is no Harry Potter, but there is J. K. Rowling. She was a single mother living in the real world with almost no money. She might not have had a magic wand but she had the courage and faith to keep following the story she was called to write. She might not have had to face the Dark Lord Voldemort, but she had to face loneliness, rejection from publishers and a never-ending stream of critics. She faced it all without a magic wand.

None of our real life heroes had special powers. Rather, every one of their successes has a series of defeated fears behind it. Every one of their triumphs has a lifetime of actively gaining **self-knowledge**, developing **self-worth**, taking **responsibility** and then continually moving forward in faith, even when they were afraid.

Courage is learned and developed over time.

Learn to appreciate all the small – possibly tiny – steps you take in developing your courage. They all count towards your freedom.

To help you, I'm going to provide some new **meanings** around courage:

- Courage is relative.

- There is a warrior within you.

- Courage is a verb.

- There's a fine line between scared and excited.

By the end of this chapter you will be able to look at courage in a new way and see that you have everything within you that you will ever need in order to be courageous and create freedom.

"We must walk consciously only part way toward our goal, and then leap in the dark to our success."

– Henry David Thoreau

Courage is relative

You can begin to view courage with a new perspective by understanding that your most courageous moments can only be determined relative to who you are, not in comparison with anyone else.

One of my most courageous moments happened when I was in my early twenties. I'd woken up in the middle of the night and immediately felt a surge of tension and anxiety within me. I'd been suffering from panic attacks and I could feel another one coming on. On a previous occasion when I'd had that same feeling, I sat up in bed, panicked and breathing heavily. I turned on the light, waking my partner, and he leapt out of bed saying, "What should I do? What should I do?" I didn't know how to respond.

On this occasion, I stopped myself from turning on the light and waking my partner. I'd been to some sessions with a psychologist since my previous attacks and had read a couple of books on the topic. As I lay there in terror, I tried to remember all that I had learned and discussed with my psychologist. I also tried to focus on being calm rather than the 'I'm going to die' feeling – the feeling that fuels the panic.

I silently said to myself, and whoever else was listening, *'If this is the moment I die, okay. I don't want to be afraid anymore. I am not afraid anymore.'* I surrendered. I let go and waited. I kept waiting until I noticed my heartbeat slowing. I noticed the pillow under my head. I was back in my bed. After lying there a little longer, suspiciously wondering why nothing had happened and if I should still be concerned, I fell asleep.

I never had another panic attack again.

It was years before I fully understood the power and significance of what I had done. Like most people, I undervalued the courage I sourced within me that night. I hadn't taken the actions of a typical hero. I know I was just lying in my warm bed – I'm not crazy. I didn't save anyone's life. Yet I was willing to take on death. In the midst of that panic attack and surrender, I was willing to die. It felt real to me.

It was the most courageous I had ever been.

That's all that matters – that we are more courageous today than we were yesterday.

I know there will be people who read my story and dismiss it as pathetic. I don't care anymore. Worrying about what other people thought and judging myself against social standards limited my freedom for far too long.

When it's your fear, it's truly scary to you. It doesn't matter if it seems ridiculous to anyone else. I promise you there are people who are truly afraid of things that do not seem scary to you at all.

You do yourself a huge disservice when you undervalue the courage that you source to face your fears. If I had acknowledged at the time the amount of courage it took to surrender in the middle of my panic attack, then I'd have still got to where I am today, but I'd have gotten here a lot faster. I'd have reviewed that moment and thought, *'If I can do that, then what else can I do?'* Instead I diminished it.

I still reaped benefits from that experience, because I never had another panic attack. You can't do something like that in your life and not be changed. But there was so much more I could have done with my new-found sense of self if I'd been wise enough to give her the credence she deserved. Instead I diminished her because I assessed her against a socially constructed definition of courage. That would be like hiking for a week to the top of a mountain and risking death while slaying a green, fire-breathing dragon and then saying, "But that one doesn't count," because the people down in the village say that you are only courageous if you slay a red dragon!

Never underestimate the value of the personal battles you chose to face and the courage it took to do so.

Every act of courage makes you wiser and stronger. Every act of courage moves you toward your next challenge and opportunity for growth.

Every act of courage is your invitation to the universe to send you something even greater. If you minimise it, you are sending out the message that you're not ready for a bigger challenge.

There is a warrior within you

In her book *The Places that Scare You*, [29] Pema Chodron describes warriors of non-aggression. These warriors recognise that our greatest harm comes from our own aggressive and fearful minds. Those of us who have not learned to be warriors of non-aggression look to deal with our challenges in ways that will not cause us discomfort, perhaps through avoidance or numbing or making our issues about someone else. While we all want to be healed, this is not possible if we are not willing to face our fears and uncertainty.

I am always inspired when I see people engaging with their internal warrior. A few years back, my long-time friend Gretel proved she is one such warrior. After calling her a couple of times without a response, I finally heard back a couple of weeks later. She told me she had just spent the last three hours riding to the top of the mountain she was now standing on. I knew she enjoyed cycling so it was not that surprising, though I hadn't known her to do such intensive rides before. She sounded quite out of breath.

Gretel said, "I have something to tell you but I'm not sure how." After a long pause, she said, "Charlie had an affair. I've decided to leave him and we're probably going to get divorced."

I knew in that instant that being at the top of the mountain when she told me her news was no coincidence. I trusted this intuition and used it to make the situation a little lighter. In a slightly sarcastic tone, I said, "Yes, well, it's always best to ride to the top of a mountain before sharing news like that." Through a mixture of laughter and tears, Gretel responded, "I just felt embarrassed and ashamed."

Right in that moment, Gretel was engaging her internal warrior. That's what it took to engage vulnerability like that. She also needed her internal warrior to face a future that seemed more uncertain than ever. Gretel's sense of identity was of a happily married woman; someone who had life figured out. If she wasn't that person, then who was she? This was, for her, a very scary prospect. It was an identity crisis and she didn't know if she had the courage, strength or skills to deal with it. Of course, I knew she had those qualities, but it's easy to say that when you're the person watching from the sidelines.

It's also very easy to discredit someone when you have no skin in the game. Notice if you think the label 'warrior' is an exaggeration for what Gretel was that day. If you undervalue Gretel's courage, it's likely you will do the same to yourself.

Just like when I took on my fear in the middle of my panic attack, Gretel taking on her greatest fears was a battle occurring in her own mind. This can be one of the most frightening battles to face and it takes a warrior. Not everyone is willing to do it but it's important that we do because when we conquer the battles in our own minds and create freedom internally, we also create freedom externally.

The external world is always a reflection of the internal world. Often when we see people engaging in conflict around them, it's because they are unwilling or unable to deal with their inner struggle. The external challenges might look like office politics, a long, drawn-out divorce battle, a street brawl or internet trolling. Regardless of the context, these situations are typically being enacted by people who aren't willing to take on the aspects of themselves they find uncomfortable or shameful but need an outlet for their internal conflict.

Gretel was a warrior. She faced her truth, her fears and her shame. She looked toward a future that seemed more uncertain than ever and made a choice to go forward, even if it meant being vulnerable. She committed to taking **responsibility** as the co-creator of her life and to always remember her **self-worth**. To do anything less than that would be to keep herself captive and she wanted to be free. She knew in her heart that if all she did was ride to the top of a mountain and go home again, her ultimate challenge would still be waiting for her.

Gretel has gone on to have an extraordinary life for which she is so grateful. That life, while not yet existing in the physical world, was created at the top of that mountain.

Courage is a verb

Though she knew she needed to, Gretel couldn't bear to pick up the phone and share her devastating news, so she decided to first take on a challenge that seemed less scary. She rode to the top of a mountain and figured if she could do that then she could take the next step.

When it comes to building courage, some action, no matter how small, is better than none. You can't read a book on courage and expect to be courageous. You need to take action – courage is a verb. It doesn't matter if you only take baby steps, you just need to keep moving. Each action you take on those things that scare you will enhance your courage to take the next step.

There was a time that I couldn't have imagined getting on a stage and singing a song I had written myself to a few hundred people. But my experiences of singing lessons and singing at my friend's wedding, which I shared in the preface of this book, meant the notion of singing on that stage was brought into my realm of possibility. One step led to the next.

With each fear that you conquer, you expand the realm of what is possible for you, strengthening your courage element in the process. This book would never have been written if I had not first found the courage to take on what seemed, to me, to be a smaller challenge. I committed to writing a blog article every week for one year. Prior to that, I'd never written anything for public consumption; I had too much self-doubt and fear of criticism.

I spent about three days writing the first article. My need for it to be perfect meant I spent a lot of time researching and refining my words. The second, third and fourth articles took almost as long. This, of course, was not sustainable. I couldn't afford to spend so much time on the task. So I had a choice: Give up or write faster and learn to let go of perfection. I decided to find the courage to 'write and let go'. The writing needed to be completed within a day and then, no matter how imperfect I believed my writing was, I had to publish.

No matter what you create, some people will like it and some won't. Knowing this in theory did little to build my courage as a writer. But committing to writing those articles every week would teach me some things I could only learn through taking action. One time, I posted an article that I thought still needed a lot more work and I was certain it would be judged poorly. To my surprise and curiosity, the article was shared many times over and I received messages of gratitude about how the article had made a difference to my readers' lives. Yet other times I'd write an article that I thought was worthy of an award, hit send and then... nothing. Nothing! I could hear the crickets in the silence of non-response!

It was only through the action of writing each article, and overcoming my fears of doing so, that I truly understood how little control I have over the opinions of others. I mean, I *really* got it. And suddenly there wasn't much to be afraid of any more. By the time I was halfway to my goal and writing the twenty-fifth article, it was no longer a task that required a lot of courage. What had once been scary had become relatively easy and positioned me for the next thing I was called to do – writing this book. And while the writing of this book brought its own uncertainties, my experiences with writing articles meant I was willing to take those uncertainties on because I had already built some of the psychological muscles that would be required.

"There is no greater threat to the critics, cynics and fearmongers than a person who is willing to fall because she's learned how to rise."

– Brene Brown

There's a fine line between scared and excited

"It's scary," my client Joanna had said when discussing her upcoming job interview. She also knew it was an opportunity and potentially a big step forward in her career. But that's part of what made it scary – she now had something to lose.

As a coach, I'm keenly aware of the power of words and labels. There are some words that can inspire us to feel more courageous and others that can cause us to shrink back.

In Joanna's case, she was viewing the job opportunity as 'scary'. I asked her, "Is it scary or is it exciting?" She paused, thought and then said, "Both."

I questioned her further, "What happens when you tell yourself it's scary?"

Without hesitation, Joanna responded "I start freaking out."

Joanna was responding as most people do: When we call something scary, we go on high alert and we worry about all the things that could go wrong.

"What if we labelled it as 'exciting'?" I asked her. Joanna noted she felt a lot better when she framed the opportunity in this way; it actually made her look forward to it and feel more optimistic about how things would turn out.

What's interesting is the sensations of fear and excitement don't feel all that different in the body. It's actually quite easy to mix them up. They both create tension in the body and activate the mind. As Joanna explored the feelings of excitement and fear, she concluded she was experiencing both in the anticipation of the new job opportunity. In spite of feeling both, the issue previously was that she was only using one of the labels, and that label of 'scary' was fuelling her fear.

This is an issue I see in people with all kinds of opportunities, including public speaking, a job promotion or a new relationship. By simply expanding your vocabulary around the event to include 'excited' as well as 'scary', you also expand the fine line between the two, giving you greater choice in how to respond next.

"Life shrinks or expands in proportion to one's courage."

– Anais Nin

Chapter summary

- Courage is faith. It is your willingness to keep moving forward and taking on life, even when the outcome is uncertain – and the outcome is always uncertain.

- Our most courageous moments are not our external triumphs – they are the conscious, internal shifts we make to change ourselves and our lives. Every triumph has a series of defeated fears behind it.

- When we misdiagnose what it means to be courageous, we miss important opportunities to develop courage.

- Courage can be learned and developed over time by remembering that: Courage is relative; there is a warrior within you; courage requires action; and there is a fine line between scared and excited.

- If you undervalue the small successes, you won't create them. And if you don't create the small successes, you won't create the big ones.

- Personal freedom involves a constant state of growth. Your inner voice is constantly calling you to take one more step into the unknown. If you resist the call because you fear the unknown or are afraid of failing, you hold yourself captive and diminish your own freedom.

Continued action will take you from having theories about freedom to actually knowing what it really means and how it really feels when you are free.

CONCLUSION

I don't really expect anyone to be much wiser or freer from simply reading this book. I hope you had several 'a-ha' moments, I hope you felt while reading that you are not alone on your journey to creating a life of freedom, and I hope you have been inspired. To truly experience freedom and gain wisdom however, you need to take what you have learned and put it in motion.

In an interview, Joseph Campbell described a conversation he had with a student in one of his lectures:

> "I had been talking about Dante and the stages of life and so forth, through the period of maturity, then to wisdom, and this youngster comes up at the end of the lecture and says, "Doctor Campbell, you don't realise, today we go directly from what you call

infancy to wisdom." I said, "That's really wonderful. All you've missed is life." [30]

Campbell noticed that several other students also thought that wisdom consisted of knowledge obtained from books and concepts. But to quote Campbell again, "It's the integration of knowledge with life that really constitutes wisdom."

So your next step must be action. Continued action will take you from having theories about freedom to actually *knowing* what it really means and how it really feels when you are free.

If you're inspired to take massive action, do it! I'm a big fan of massive action. You'll succeed or you won't. Either way, you'll learn and you'll be one step closer to living with freedom.

I'm also a fan of *any* action, no matter how small, that empowers or frees you to create the vision you have for yourself.

> *"Most people overestimate what they can do in one year and underestimate what they can do in ten years."*
>
> **– Bill Gates**

Too often, people are overwhelmed by the thought of how much they think they need to do so ultimately they end up doing nothing. Others take massive action but then fizzle out as their **energy** and motivation wane when they don't achieve their desired results as fast as they want.

Find the right balance – something that stretches you to learn and grow and achieve more than before, but in a way that's sustainable and will create ongoing changes in the long term.

And then, keep going! This is your life we're talking about, so keep taking action every day toward your life of freedom.

Some days you will have setbacks or feel like you have let yourself down. But those things are really just a blip in a much longer journey. Experience the blips, learn from them, but don't let them stop you. You need to keep going so you can move to the next learning experience – the next piece of wisdom on your journey to greater freedom.

"Do one thing every day that scares you."

– Eleanor Roosevelt

Take action to increase your **self-knowledge** through experience. Become conscious of all of the **meanings** you create about your experiences. Do things that prove beyond doubt that you consider yourself to be of high **self-worth**. Commit to managing your **energy** levels to sustain you through all your endeavours. Give yourself time to regularly create peace and **calm** in your mind and your environment. And take **responsibility** for all of the results you are creating in your life.

You have no guarantee of how life will unfold. But you can be free by moving forward with **courage** and faith and taking action anyway.

"Be a doer, not a dreamer."

– Shonda Rhimes

ACKNOWLEDGEMENTS

Seven Freedom Elements was many years in the making. Throughout that time, virtually everyone I've interacted with has contributed in some way. There were also some people who were particularly supportive throughout the journey from concept to published book and I'm so grateful.

To all my clients who I've had the privilege to journey with: Every time you show up to claim another piece of your freedom, I'm in awe and feel privileged. Thank you for being my inspiration. Thank you for all you do for yourself and for the greater good.

To Avril: You've been a constant source of support, honest yet non-judgemental feedback and personal development. Moreover, you've been a constant; for years, our weekly conversations are always something I look forward to and provide a valuable source of connection and love.

To my editors and proof readers: Jacqui Pretty of the Grammar Factory, thank you so much for your insights and expertise on writing; things moved much faster after I found you. Caroline, your writing and content expertise never ceased to inspire, challenge and amaze me. Alex Mitchell, thank you for your skills, insights and guidance. Avril, Annette, Magali and Mum, your time, interest, encouragement and feedback were invaluable and I am eternally grateful.

To my publishing team: Morgan James Publishing – Thank you for believing in this book and your invaluable expertise as you guided me through the publishing journey. Julia Kuris of Designerbility – I love the cover we created! Thank you for your insight, expertise, creativity, professionalism and patience. Vivienne at Excite Print – thank you for turning the digital files into a physical reality and guiding me through the process. Douglas Williams – thank you for your patience and excellent work on the internal design.

To my BFFs: Sarah, Avril, Clare, Karina, Caroline, Helen, Madeleine, Chizu and Nikki - you are all proof of the value a genuine female friend adds to the wellbeing of the female spirit. I am so blessed to have all of you.

To my BMFs: Kon, thank you for the myriad of ways you provided encouragement and support for the creation of this book. I am so grateful. Glenn, your courage and determination are inspirational.

To the many who have shown their support: Mike, Phil, Sharon, Mark, Kate, Jo, Graeme, John, Gae, Jen Sincero and the Badass group, Kerry, Karen, Simone, Louise, Nikki, Richard, Sarah and everyone who provided tips, feedback and encouragement. I'm so grateful.

To my parents, Chris, Kirsten, Brodie and Jack: I love you.

WORKS CITED

1. N. Burton, *Hide and Seek: The Psychology of Self-deception*, Acheron Press, 2012.

2. R. B. Cialdini, *Influence - The Psychology of Persuasion* (Revised Edition), New York: HarperCollins Publishers, 2007.

3. H. Lerner, *The Dance of Connection*, HarperCollins, 2009.

4. B. Katie, *Loving What Is*, New York: Penguin Random House, 2002.

5. A. Solomon, "How the worst moments in our lives make us who we are," March 2014. [Online]. Available: http://www.ted.com/talks/andrew_solomon_how_the_worst_moments_in_our_lives_make_us_who_we_are. [Accessed 2015].

6. V. E. Frankl, *Man's Search for Meaning* (Fourth Edition), Boston: Beacon Press, 1992.

7. M. S. Peck, *The Road Less Travelled*, Simon and Schuster, 2012.

8. A. Walker, *The Color Purple*, Phoenix: Orion Books, 2014.

9. C. McHugh, "The Art of Being Yourself: Caroline McHugh at TEDxMiltonKeynesWomen," [Online]. Available: http://tedxtalks.ted.com/video/The-Art-of-Being-Yourself-Carol. [Accessed May 2016].

10. B. Brown, *Rising Strong*, Ebury Publishing, 2015.

11. C. Myss, *Self Esteem: Your Fundamental Power* [audio recording], Sounds True, 2002.

12. S. Pressfield, *The War of Art*, New York: Black Irish Entertainment LLC, 2002.

13. K. McGonigal, *The Willpower Instinct*, Penguin Group, 2012.

14. R. Simmons, *Success through Stillness*, New York: Penguin Random House, 2014.

15. World Health Organisation. [Online]. Available: http://www.who.int/mental_health. [Accessed 9 October 2016].

16. A. Solomon, "Depression, the secret we share (TED talks)," 2013. [Online]. Available: https://www.ted.com/talks/andrew_solomon_depression_the_secret_we_share. [Accessed 2016].

17. C. Northrup, *Goddesses Never Age: The Secret Prescription*, Hay House, 2015.

18. M. Oaten and K. Cheng, "Longitudinal gains in self-regulation from regular physical exercise," British Journal of Health Psychology, vol. 11, no. 4, pp. 717-733, 2006.

19. M. Robbins, *Stop Saying You're Fine: Discover a More Powerful You*, Random House, 2011.

20. F. Batmanghelidj, *Water: For Health, for Healing, for Life: You're not Sick, You're Thirsty!*, New York: Warner Books Inc., 2003.

21. R. Foster, "Why do we sleep?," June 2013. [Online]. Available: http://www.ted.com/talks/russell_foster_why_do_we_sleep. [Accessed 2015].

22. J. Iliff, "One more reason to get a good night's sleep," September 2014. [Online]. Available: http://www.ted.com/talks/jeff_iliff_one_more_reason_to_get_a_good_night_s_sleep. [Accessed 2015].

23. J. Bolte Taylor, "My Stroke of Insight," 2008. [Online]. Available: https://www.ted.com/talks/jill_bolte_taylor_s_powerful_stroke_of_insight. [Accessed 2015].

24. S. Harris, *Waking Up: Searching for Spirituality Without Religion*, London: Penguin Random House, 2014.

25. P. Chodron and A. Walker, Pema Chodron and Alice Walker in Conversation: On the Meaning of Suffering and the Mystery of Joy [audio recording], Sounds True, 2014.

26. J. J. Arnett, *Emerging Adulthood; The Winding Road from the Late Teens Through the Twenties*, Oxford University Press, 2014.

27. O. James, *They F*** You Up: How to Survive Family Life*, Bloomsbury Publishing Plc, 2007.

28. B. Ware, *The Top Five Regrets of the Dying*, Hay House Inc., 2012.

29. P. Chodron, *The Places that Scare You: A Guide to Fearlessness in Difficult Times*, Boston: Shambhala Publications, 2001.

30. J. Campbell and M. Toms, *The Wisdom of Joseph Campbell - In Conversation with Michael Toms* [audio recording], Hay House Inc., 2005.

ABOUT THE AUTHOR

Kylie Zeal is a Professional Certified Coach. She is passionate about people creating the freedom to live their most inspired lives and contributing to a healthier world. After a decade of coaching individuals and facilitating groups, Kylie was clear that there were key elements people needed to develop if they wanted to experience true freedom in their lives. This knowledge became the basis of her book, Seven Freedom Elements.

Kylie spent two years managing a research project exploring the benefits of coaching. At the completion of the project, she facilitated coach training across Australia. Kylie has a bachelor of Social Science with majors in psychology and sociology.

Please visit the website at: SevenFreedomElements.com

Morgan James
Speakers Group

We connect Morgan James published authors with live and online events and audiences who will benefit from their expertise.

Printed in the USA
CPSIA information can be obtained
at www.ICGtesting.com
JSHW022322140824
68134JS00019B/1244

9 781683 505372